# Handbook of *Australian*
# Wildlife

A *Steve Parish* CONCISE GUIDE

# Contents

p. 66

p. 196

p. 172

p. 119

p. 57

p. 33

p. 74

p. 182

p. 238

3

# Australian wildlife

Australia, the world's smallest continent, is home to a remarkable variety of wild animals. It is renowned for its unusual animals, many of which are not found in other countries. These amazing creatures have developed in isolation over millions of years. Each one has a body and lifestyle suited to Australian conditions.

This guide introduces the main groups of native species found in Australia and its coastal waters. Profiles of familiar and uncommon species will help novice wildlife watchers learn how to identify animals in the wild.

# Abbreviations

| | | | | |
|---|---|---|---|---|
| **mm** | = millimetres | **e.g.** | = for example |
| **cm** | = centimetres | **sp.** | = species (singular) |
| **m** | = metre | **spp.** | = species (plural) |
| **g** | = gram | **Aust.** | = Australia |
| **kg** | = kilogram | **Tas.** | = Tasmania |
| **HB** | = length of head + body to vent | **Qld** | = Queensland |
| | | **WA** | = Western Australia |
| **HBT** | = length of head + body + tail | **NSW** | = New South Wales |
| **T** | = length of tail from vent to tip | **ACT** | = Australian Capital Territory |
| | | **NT** | = Northern Territory |
| ♀ | = female | **Vic.** | = Victoria |
| ♂ | = male | **G** | = Glossary |

# Australian vegetation

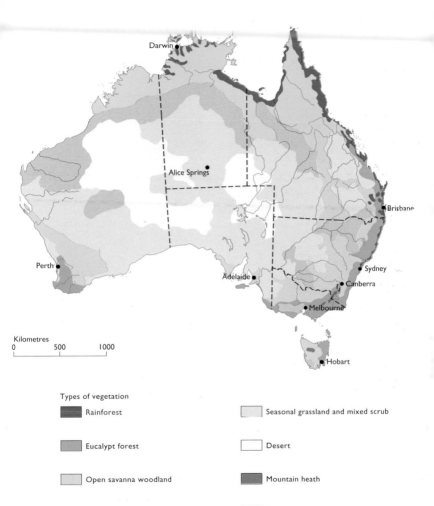

Types of vegetation

Rainforest

Eucalypt forest

Open savanna woodland

Open grassland and low-tree savanna

Seasonal grassland and mixed scrub

Desert

Mountain heath

Coastal swamp forest and heath

5

# Wildlife habitats

Rainforests

Eucalypt forests and woodlands

Shrublands

Hummock grasslands

Desert

Wetlands

A habitat is the place where an animal finds the things it needs to survive. Australia's climate, vegetation, natural and human-made features create thousands of different wildlife habitats.

Parks and gardens

Farmland

Estuaries and mangroves

Sandy shores and bays

Coral reefs and cays

Rocky shores and reefs

# Naming animals

**Common name**
An animal may have a common name that can vary from place to place. e.g. Gould's Goanna or Sand Monitor. .

**Scientific name**
It also has a two-word scientific name that is used worldwide. This is written in italics in reverse order to English names. e.g. *Varanus gouldii*

IAN MORRIS

**What is a species?**
Animals of the same species can breed with each other and produce fertile offspring.

**These wombats are two species.**

The Southern Hairy-nosed Wombat (*Lasiorhinus latifrons*) and the Northern Hairy-nosed Wombat (*Lasiorhinus krefftii*) do not interbreed.

**These birds are one species.**

The Eastern Reef Egret (*Egretta sacra*) can be grey or white. The two colour phases breed with each other. Chicks of both colours may be seen in one nest.

# Grouping animals

Animals are classified or sorted into groups according to their body structures and how their bodies work. Each classification level describes the features a group of animals have in common. The details become more specific at each level until only one kind of animal fits the description. The system helps scientists describe and identify animals, and to see if and how different animals are related.

**An example of classification**

Common name: Red Kangaroo

Scientific name: *Macropus rufus*

| LEVEL | EXAMPLE | FEATURES |
|---|---|---|
| Kingdom | Animalia | Living, multi-celled things excluding plants, bacteria, fungi |
| Phylum | Chordata | Animals with nerve chord along back |
| Subphylum | Vertebrata | Chordates with jointed backbones |
| Class | Mammalia | Vertebrates with mammary glands |
| Subclass | Marsupialia | Mammals with pouch where newborns develop |
| Order | Diprodontia | Marsupials with two lower incisors |
| Family | Macropodidae | Diprodonts with long feet and powerful hind legs |
| Genus | Macropus | Typical macropods |
| Species | rufus | Red-coloured |

# Watching wildlife

Not all animals are easy to see or find. Many are small, well camouflaged or only active at night. The more you know about an animal's appearance and behaviour, the more likely it is you will find one in the wild.

## Where to start

- visit zoos, wildlife sanctuaries, aquariums
- look in your garden or local park
- go on a guided walk in a national park
- check out a rockpool at low tide

PETER SLATER

## In the field

- hold still and see what comes to you
- move slowly and quietly
- don't approach animals head-on
- try to blend in with the surroundings
- wear appropriate clothing and footwear
- use binoculars, a magnifying glass, a camera
- try spotlighting at night
- use your eyes, ears and nose

## Look for:

- movement
- tracks
- animal droppings
- scratches on ground or trees
- fur, feathers, shells, cast-off skins
- piles of dirt or rubble in front of holes

# Record your sightings

Date: 24 May, 2003
Time: 8:30 p.m.
Place: 77 Grevillea Rd, Upper Swan, W.A.

Weather: Warm and humid; rain 5–6 p.m.
Observer: Chris Menindii

black
white
white

Length HB = 6.4 cm
Notes: Call <u>koop-koop</u> or <u>coo-coo</u>. Found frog on sandy soil near swampy area in horse paddock. Underside of first finger of hand had black spikes. Breeding male?
WESTERN SPOTTED FROG <u>Heleioporus albopunctatus</u>

Make notes and drawings in the field. Use your observations and reference books to work out an animal's name. Eliminate some species by habitat and range.

## Things to note:

**Size** – compare to an animal you know

**Shape** – of body, head, legs, eyes etc.

**Colour** – of body parts

**Voice** – describe calls animal makes

**Habitat** – describe the animal's surroundings

**Behaviour** – what is the animal doing?

## Be aware

Few Australian animals deliberately attack humans; however, they will defend themselves if threatened or provoked. Their bites, stings, scratches or kicks can range from irritating to fatal. Most injuries occur when people try to handle or kill animals.

Saltwater (Estuarine) Crocodile (p.113)

Blue-ringed Octopus (p.287)

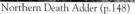

Northern Death Adder (p.148)

IAN MORRIS

# Mammals

An animal is a mammal if it:

- has mammary glands producing milk to feed young
- has a backbone and skull
- is warm-blooded and has a four-chambered heart
- has lungs and breathes air
- has hair or fur
- has limbs, usually four

## Where and when

- go spotlighting at night for possums
- dawn and dusk in grassy bushland for wallabies
- visit a coastal headland from June to October to see migrating whales

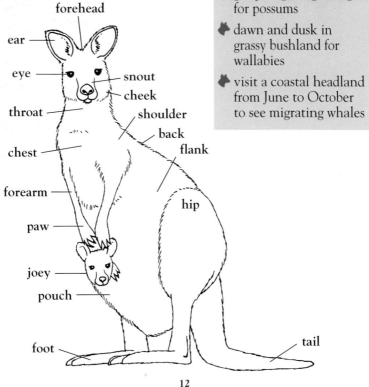

forehead

ear

eye

snout

cheek

throat

shoulder

back

chest

flank

forearm

hip

paw

joey

pouch

foot

tail

12

# Mammal groups

Mammals are divided into three main groups according to the way they produce young.

**Monotreme mammals lay soft-shelled eggs. The tiny babies are not fully developed.**

| | |
|---|---|
| Monotremata | Platypus, Echidnas |

**Marsupial mammals give birth to tiny, partially developed young. A newborn continues development attached to a nipple inside a pouch or fold of skin on its mother's belly.**

| | |
|---|---|
| Polyprotodonta | quolls, Numbat, dunnarts, bandicoots, devil, bilbies |
| Diprotodonta | wombats, Koala, possums, wallabies, kangaroos |

**Placental mammals give birth to well-developed young that suckle milk when hungry.**

| | |
|---|---|
| Chiroptera | flying-foxes, bats |
| Rodentia | rats, mice |
| Pinnipedia | seals, sea-lions |
| Sirenia | Dugong |
| Cetacea | dolphins, whales |
| Carnivora | Dingo |

 # Platypus

*Ornithorhynchus anatinus* (= duck-like bird-bill)

PETER MARSACK

**Length:** HBT: ♀ 40 ♂ 55 cm

**Weight:** ♀ 700 ♂ 2000 g

**Identification:** Cat-sized, freshwater mammal with smooth, brown fur. Has leathery bill, no visible ears, flattened body, broad tail, webbed feet. Swimming, makes a V-shaped bow-wave.

**Where found:** In or near fresh water along east coast Aust.; Tas.

**Habits:** Active at dawn and dusk. Catches small animals underwater, stores them in cheek pouches, surfaces to eat. Digs rest burrows in river bank. Female lays two rubbery eggs, 17 mm in diameter, in nest burrow, incubates[G] 2 weeks. Feeds young on milk from patches on her belly for 4–5 months.

**Notes:** Male can inject venom[G] through spurs on ankles. Baby has milk teeth, but loses them at weaning[G].

**Status:** Vulnerable. Disappears when habitat altered.

**Similar species:** Water Rat has visible ears and "dog-paddles" when swimming.

 **HABITAT** CREEKS & RIVERS

 **FOOD** WATER ANIMALS

# Short-beaked Echidna

*Tachyglossus aculeatus* (= spiny fast-tongue)

**Length:** HB 30–45 cm

**Weight:** 2–7 kg

**Identification:** Cat-sized, spine-covered, long-snouted ground animal, with powerful claws and tiny tail.

**Where found:** Aust. and Tas.

**Habits:** Active at night and on dull winter days. Claws into ant and termite nests, pulls out insects with sticky tongue. Female lays one egg, incubates it for 10 days in her pouch, suckles young for 12 weeks (in pouch, then in burrow).

**Notes:** Male has spurs, but no venom. Digs into ground or wedges into hollow when threatened. "Trains" of several males follow one female, hoping to mate with her. Droppings contain soil.

**Status:** Secure. Common.

**Similar species:** None.

**HABITAT**
NEAR FOOD
SOURCES

**FOOD**
ANTS &
TERMITES

# Brush-tailed Phascogale

*Phascogale tapoatafa* (= pouched-weasel called by Aborigines *tapoatafa*)

**Length:** HB ♀ 18 ♂ 20 cm; T ♀ 19 ♂ 21 cm

**Weight:** ♀ 160 ♂ 230 g

**Identification:** Large-rat-sized tree-dweller, with soft grey body fur, long bushy black tail. Runs up and down trunks, on and under branches, can leap up to 2 m between trees.

**Where found:** Open coastal forest around Aust.

**Habits:** Spends day in tree hollow, at night hunts insects and small mammals. May eat nectar. Female carries 3–8 young on nipples for 7 weeks, then leaves and feeds them in nest for 13 weeks.

**Notes:** Can rotate hindfoot 180° to climb up or down. Alarmed, taps forefeet on branch. All males die after mating (from stress-related illnesses, or are taken by predators). Females survive to give birth to new generation.

**Status:** Rare. Threatened by habitat destruction, cats, foxes.

**Similar species:** Endangered, rare Red-tailed Phascogale has upper part of tail rust-red.

**HABITAT** COASTAL FORESTS

**FOOD** INSECTS & SMALL LIFE

# Yellow-footed Antechinus

*Antechinus flavipes* (= yellow-footed hedgehog-like* animal)

**Length:** HB ♀ 10.5 ♂ 12 cm; T ♀ 8.5 ♂ 10 cm

**Weight:** ♀ 3.5 ♂ 5.6 g

**Identification:** Looks like large mouse with big ears, longish snout. Has grey head, light rings around eyes, reddish rump, belly and sides, yellow-brown feet. Black tail tip.

**Where found:** Many habitats, including gardens, from north-eastern Qld to southwestern WA.

**Habits:** Spends day in nest under log or leaves. At night hunts insects, house mice, other small animals. Moves in quick rushes, searches leaf litter, climbs.

**Notes:** May enter houses looking for mice and spiders. In spring, males mate (act may last up to 12 hours) then die. Females carry up to 10 young for 5 weeks, then suckle them in nest for 15 weeks.

**Status:** Secure. Common. Often caught by cats.

**Similar species:** Brown Antechinus is grey-brown above, paler below, lacks light eye-rings.

* Damp antechinus fur looks spiky.

**HABITAT**
WOODED
AREAS

**FOOD**
INSECTS &
SMALL LIFE

# Fat-tailed Dunnart

*Sminthopsis crassicaudata* (= fat-tailed mouse-like animal)

**Length:** HB 6–9 cm; T 4–7cm

**Weight:** 10–20 g

**Identification:** Large-mouse-sized, grey-brown hunter with large ears, fat tail. Large eyes in dark eye-rings, very pointed muzzle, long, narrow hindfeet.

**Where found:** Woodlands, plains, farmlands across southern and central Aust.

**Habits:** Shelters during day in nest in hole, or under log. Hunts at night for insects and other small animals. Usually 5 young, carried in well-developed pouch for 5 weeks, fed in nest for 5 weeks.

**Notes:** Several may share nest in cold weather. Fat in tail is winter food reserve. May have increased range with clearing of land.

**Status:** Secure. Common.

**Similar species:** Stripe-faced Dunnart is a fat-tailed, inland species with dark facial stripe.

**HABITAT** WOODLANDS & PLAINS

**FOOD** INSECTS & SMALL LIFE

# Kultarr

*Antechinomys laniger* (= woolly-furred mouse-like animal)

**Length:** HB 8.5 cm; T 12–13 cm

**Weight:** 20–30 g

**Identification:** Large-mouse-sized, large-eared hunter with long hindlegs, long, tuft-ended tail. Brown-grey above, white below. Bounds rather than hops.

**Where found:** Desert inland plains, stony and sandy land.

**Habits:** Shelters during day in a burrow. Hunts at night for insects, spiders and other small animals. 6–8 young carried by female, protected by fold of skin on belly, for 4 weeks, then left in nest for 9 weeks. Later ride on mother's back while she hunts. Weaned at 12 weeks.

**Notes:** An active desert predator.

M & I MORCOMBE

**Status:** Probably secure. Vulnerable to habitat changes.

**Similar species:** None.

**HABITAT** INLAND DESERT

**FOOD** INSECTS & SMALL LIFE

# Spotted-tailed Quoll

*Dasyurus maculatus* (= spotted hairy-tailed animal)

IAN MORRIS

**Length:** HB small ♀ 35 large ♂ 76 cm; T ♀ 34 ♂ 55 cm

**Weight:** ♀ to 4 kg, ♂ to 7 kg

**Identification:** Small-dog-sized hunter with brown, white-spotted body and long, spotted tail. Bounds on ground, climbs trees.

**Where found:** In isolated forest areas down east coast of Aust., and in Tas.

**Habits:** Prey ranges from insects to small wallabies, also carrion[G]. Droppings made in special places in territory. Mating lasts up to 8 hours. Female develops pouch, 5 young remain there for 7 weeks, fed in nest 6 weeks.

**Notes:** Largest marsupial predator[G] on mainland. Male feeds female and young.

**Status:** Disappearing through habitat destruction, competition with fox, cat.

**Similar species:** Northern and Eastern Quolls unspotted tails; Eastern Quoll only rarely recorded on mainland.

**HABITAT**
FOREST, WOODLAND

**FOOD**
LIVE ANIMALS, CARRION

# Tasmanian Devil

*Sarcophilus harrisii* (= Harris's flesh-eater)

**Length:** HB ♀ 57 ♂ 65 cm; T ♀ 24 ♂ 26 cm

**Weight:** ♀ 7 ♂ 9 kg

**Identification:** Black scavenger with white markings on chest and rump. Looks like a medium-sized, bulky dog.

**Where found:** All over Tas., especially in northeast.

**Habits:** Spends day in den. Dusk to dawn hunts for dead animals, insects, small mammals. Can climb trees. 2–4 young born April, carried in rear-opening pouch for 16 weeks, then left in den. Young on own at 40 weeks.

**Notes:** Largest living marsupial carnivore". Lived on mainland until around 400 years ago. Group feeding at carcass may squabble loudly. Not dangerous to humans or their animals.

**Status:** Secure, common in Tas.

**Similar species:** None.

**HABITAT**
ALL OVER
TASMANIA

**FOOD**
LIVE ANIMALS,
CARRION

# Numbat

*Myrmecobius fasciatus* (= striped ant-eater)

M & I MORCOMBE

**Where found:** Survives in a few isolated eucalypt forests in southwestern WA.

**Habits:** Active during day. Shelters and sleeps in a hollow fallen log. May dig a burrow. Feeds on termites, scratched and licked with long, slender tongue from under rotting wood or surface tunnels.

**Length:** HB 24 cm; T 17 cm

**Weight:** 460–484 g

**Identification:** Cat-sized, red-brown marsupial with dark rump striped with white. Narrow head, sharp muzzle, dark stripe through eye. Long tail "bottle-brushes" when the owner is active.

**Notes:** Once found across southern Australia from western NSW to coast of WA. 4 young born January, carried for 5 months, then fed in nest 5 months.

**Status:** Rare and endangered. Threatened by habitat loss, foxes, fires.

**Similar species:** None.

HABITAT
EUCALYPT
FORESTS

FOOD
TERMITES

# Marsupial Mole

*Notoryctes typhlops* (= blind southern digger)

STANLEY BREEDEN

**Length:** HB 12–16 cm; T 2 cm

**Weight:** 40–70 g

**Identification:** Rat-sized, burrowing marsupial with golden, silky fur. Blind. Horny shield on nose; no visible ears. 2 bladelike front claws are used for digging and gripping prey.

**Where found:** Sandy deserts from central Aust. to north-west coast of WA.

**Habits:** The Marsupial Mole lives in sand, digging tunnels which collapse behind it. Eats insects found underground; may surface after rain. Female has rear-opening pouch and two nipples.

**Notes:** Little known. Adapted to life underground, the Marsupial Mole looks very like the true moles, which are unrelated placental mammals.

**Status:** Not known. It is very rarely seen.

**Similar species:** None.

**HABITAT**
SANDY
DESERTS

**FOOD**
BURROWING
ANIMALS

# Southern Brown Bandicoot

*Isoodon obesulus* (= equal-toothed* rather fat animal)

**Length:** HB ♀ 30 ♂ 33 cm; T ♀ 11 ♂ 12 cm

**Weight:** ♀ 700 ♂ 850 g

**Identification:** Cat-sized, ground-living bandicoot with pointed muzzle, humped back, thin tail. Grey-brown above and white below. Bounds and gallops when moving fast.

**Where found:** Across southwestern and southeastern Aust. and in Tas., in areas with sandy soil and low ground cover. Increases after low-level fires renew vegetation.

**Habits:** Solitary<sup>G</sup>. Shelters in nest on ground during day, feeds on insects, earthworms and fungi at night, leaving conical holes in ground. Up to six young are carried in a rear-opening pouch, then weaned at around 9 weeks.

**Notes:** Needs home range of up to 7 hectares to supply food needs. Individuals' ranges may overlap if food plentiful.

**Status:** Becoming less common as its habitat disappears.

**Similar species:** The Long-nosed Bandicoot, found in the eastern part of this species' range, has longer, pointed muzzle, much larger ears and white feet.

* Refers to the length of the incisor teeth.

JIRI LOCHMAN

**HABITAT** HEATH & SCRUB

**FOOD** FUNGI & SMALL LIFE

24

# Greater Bilby

*Macrotis lagotis* (= liura-eared large-eared animal)

**Length:** HB ♀ 34 ♂ 42 cm; T ♀ 24 ♂ 25 cm

**Weight:** ♀ 950 ♂ 1750 g

**Identification:** Small-cat-sized burrowing marsupial with long ears, long muzzle, soft grey fur. Long, black, white-tipped tail.

**Where found:** Desert areas of central Aust. with little free surface water.

**Habits:** Shelters during day in a burrow that may be 3 m long and nearly 2 m deep. Gets moisture from insects, seeds, fungi; digs feeding holes 10 cm deep. Droppings may contain sand. 2 young stay in the rear-opening pouch for about 11 weeks, then are left in burrow.

**Notes:** Once found in dry areas across southern Australia. Threatened by grazing, fire, rabbits and foxes.

**Status:** Rare and endangered.

**Similar species:** The Lesser Bilby is much smaller. It is almost certainly extinct.

**HABITAT** SANDY DESERTS

**FOOD** INSECTS & SEEDS

# Common Wombat

*Vombatus ursinus* (= bear-like wombat)

**Length:** HB 90–115 cm; T 25 mm

**Weight:** 22–39 kg

**Identification:** Size of a large, stocky dog. A ground-living burrower, with a rounded outline, large head, naked nose and short ears. Grey to brown, coarse fur.

**Where found:** Coastal ranges, forest and woodland from northeastern NSW to southeastern SA.

**Habits:** Night-active and solitary. Several burrows will be dug in an area. Eats native grasses, shrubs, roots. In winter, may bask⁶ or feed in daytime. Female carries one young in her rear-opening pouch for 6 months; it follows her for another 11 months.

**Notes:** Not protected in some areas of eastern Victoria. Large, rectangular droppings are left on logs and rocks. Major burrows may be up to 20 m long, with several chambers and entrances.

**Status:** Probably secure, but range decreasing.

**Similar species:** Northern and Southern Hairy-nosed Wombats are very rare. They have softer fur and hairy noses.

HABITAT
WOODLANDS
& FORESTS

FOOD
GRASSES
& SHRUBS

# Koala

*Phascolarctos cinereus* (= ash-coloured pouched bear)

**Length:** HB ♀ 69 ♂ 78 cm

**Weight:** ♀ 5 ♂ 12 kg

**Identification:** Medium-dog-sized, tree-living marsupial. Has big-bellied body, round face, round furry ears, flattened nose and strong limbs. Fur is grey-brown and woolly.

**Where found:** In remaining eucalypt forest in eastern Aust.

**Habits:** Night-active and solitary. Usually seen in eucalypt trees. The low energy content of its eucalypt leaf diet means a Koala sleeps up to 20 hours out of every 24. Female carries 1 young in rear-opening pouch for 6 months, then on her back for a further 6 months.

**Notes:** Southern Koalas are larger than northern ones. Once hunted for fur

(to extinction in some areas). Vulnerable[G] to dogs when changing trees at night. Also threatened by disease and by bushfires.

**Status:** Probably secure. Common in suitable forest, but disappears with habitat.

**Similar species:** None.

**HABITAT** EUCALYPT FORESTS

**FOOD** EUCALYPT LEAVES

# Common Ringtail Possum

*Pseudocheirus peregrinus* (= wandering false-hand*)

**Length:** HB 30–35 cm; T 30–35 cm

**Weight:** 700–1100 g

**Identification:** Small-cat-sized possum. Each short ear has a white patch behind it. The long, prehensile, white-tipped tail, with a naked area beneath, is used as a fifth limb. Colour varies from copper to grey. Makes a soft, high, twittering call.

**Where found:** Down east coast from Cape York Peninsula to Tas., in areas with trees and shrubs; in gardens.

**Habits:** Spends day in a ball-shaped, leaf-lined nest in a tree hollow or dense foliage. At night eats leaves and flowers. Male and female stay together for breeding season. Two young are carried in the female's pouch for 4 months, then left in nest for 2 months. Both parents care for the young.

**Notes:** Can digest eucalypt leaves. Soft droppings are produced in nest during day, eaten and extra nourishment extracted. Fond of rosebuds.

**Status:** Secure. Common in suitable habitat.

**Similar species:** Western Ringtail Possum, found only in south–western WA, is considered rare, endangered.

* The tail serves as another hand.

**HABITAT** FORESTS & TOWNS

**FOOD** LEAVES & FLOWERS

# Common Brushtail Possum

*Trichosurus vulpecula* (= little fox-like hairy-tail)

**Length:** HB 35–55 cm;
T 24–40 cm

**Weight:** ♀ 2.4 ♂ 2.9 kg

**Identification:** Cat-sized tree-living possum with foxy face, long oval ears and copper-coloured to grey fur. Bushy tail has a short naked area underneath. Agile climber, which sits upright and holds food in its paws.

**Where found:** All over Aust., in many habitats.

**Habits:** Spends day in hollow tree, cave or roof of building. At night eats leaves, flowers, fruit. Male marks territory with chin, chest and anal<sup>G</sup> glands. Breeds autumn and spring. Female carries one young for 4–5 months in pouch, then for 2 months on back. Coughing, hissing calls.

**Notes:** Once hunted for fur. Queensland has a short-haired copper form, Tasmania a larger, woolly, dark grey form.

**Status:** Secure. Common in forests and towns.

**Similar species:** Mountain Brushtail Possum has short rounded ears; tail has long naked area underneath.

**HABITAT**
FORESTS
& TOWNS

**FOOD**
LEAVES, FRUIT,
FLOWERS

# Spotted Cuscus

*Spilocuscus maculatus* (= spotted spotted-cuscus)

**Length:** HB 35–58 cm; T 31–43 cm

**Weight:** 1.5–5 kg

**Identification:** Large-cat-sized, usually slow-moving tree-dweller. Round, bare-skinned face which may flush reddish, large round eyes, tiny ears. The prehensile[G] tail is two-thirds naked underneath. Male is blotched grey and white above, female is grey.

**Where found:** Rainforests of Cape York Peninsula, north of Coen, Qld.

**Habits:** Spends day sleeping on branch or in leaves. At night, eats leaves, fruits, flowers. Large canine[G] teeth suggest some animal food. Males may be aggressive towards each other. Usually 1 young, carried in mother's pouch, then on her back.

**Notes:** Can travel across bare ground to reach rainforest fragments. May make sleeping platform of leaves and twigs.

**Status:** Vulnerable. Needs suitable habitat for survival.

**Similar species:** Southern Common Cuscus is more possum-like, with longer snout, larger ears and stripe on back.

**HABITAT**
N.E. QLD
RAINFOREST

**FOOD**
LEAVES &
FLOWERS

# Leadbeater's Possum

*Gymnobelideus leadbeateri* (= Leadbeater's naked* glider)

**Length:** HB 15–17 cm;
T 14.5–18 cm

**Weight:** 100 (spring)–166 (autumn) g

**Identification:** Shy, rat-sized possum, grey to brown above with dark stripe from face down back. Long tail broadens at tip. Active leaper.

**Where found:** Only in mountain forests of Vic.'s central highlands.

**Habits:** Active at night. Lives in colonies of up to 8, consisting of a breeding pair and offspring, which nest together in tree hollow. Feeds on insects, spiders found beneath bark, and tree sap. Female carries 1–2 young in her pouch for over 3 months. They leave the nest at 4 months of age.

**Notes:** Group membership signalled by scent. Group defends territory of up to 2 ha, will mob predator attacking colony member. This species was not sighted 1909–1961.

**Status:** Endangered. 75% of its habitat is in timber-production forests and only 3% in nature reserves. (Suitable nest holes are only found in trees over 120 years old.)

**Similar species:** Sugar Glider has gliding membranes[G], and its tail does not broaden.

* Refers to lack of gliding membranes.

**HABITAT**
MOUNTAIN
FORESTS

**FOOD**
SMALL LIFE,
TREE SAP

# Eastern Pygmy-possum

*Cercartetus nanus* (= dwarf cercartetus*)

**Habits:** Solitary. Spends day in hollow. At night eats pollen, nectar (gathered with brush-tipped tongue), fruits and insects. Female carries 4 young in her pouch for 4 weeks, then feeds them in a bark nest for 5 weeks.

**Length:** HB 7–11 cm; T 7.5–10.5 cm

**Weight:** 15–43 g

**Identification:** Mouse-sized possum with fat-based, prehensile tail. Fawn above, white below.

**Where found:** Down eastern coast from southern Qld to eastern SA, including Tas., in rainforest, eucalypts and heaths.

**Notes:** Becomes torpid[G] in cold weather, using up fat stored in the base of the tail.

**Status:** Secure. Common, but seldom seen.

**Similar species:** Little Pygmy-possum, mainly in Tas., is smaller, with grey belly. Western Pygmy-possum found in southeastern SA and southwestern WA.

* The meaning of this is unknown.

**HABITAT** FOREST & HEATHLAND

**FOOD** NECTAR & INSECTS

# Feathertail Glider

*Acrobates pygmaeus* (= pygmy acrobat)

**Length:** HB 6.5–8 cm, T 7–8 cm

**Weight:** 10–14 g

**Identification:** Mouse-sized glider. Long tail has fringe of hair on either side. Gliding membranes between elbows and knees. Grey above, white below.

**Where found:** Forests and woodlands of eastern Aust.

**Habits:** Active at night. Feeds on nectar with brush-tipped tongue, also on pollen and insects. Groups feed and nest together in tree hollows. 3–4 young carried in pouch for 9 weeks, fed in nest for 5 weeks. Female may carry reserve embryos[G], which develop once larger young have been weaned.

**Notes:** World's smallest gliding mammal. Pads under toes, sharp claws and prehensile tail aid climbing.

**Status:** Probably secure. Found in disappearing old forests.

**Similar species:** None. The only small tree-dweller with a feather-like tail.

**HABITAT**
EASTERN
WOODLANDS

**FOOD**
NECTAR,
INSECTS

# Sugar Glider

*Petaurus breviceps* (= short-headed rope-dancer)

**Length:** HB 16–21 cm; T 16.5–21 cm

**Weight:** ♀ 95 ♂ 160 g

**Identification:** Rat-sized glider, blue-grey to brown-grey above with dark stripe from forehead to middle of back; pale below. The membrane stretching from the fifth finger to the first toe on each side of the body is used to glide between trees.

**Where found:** In coastal forests and patches of woodland from Kimberley, WA, across north, then down to southeastern SA and Tas.

**Habits:** Active at night. Lives in colonies of up to 7 adults and their young in tree hollows. Feeds on tree sap, nectar, pollen, insects. Female carries 2 young in pouch for 2–3 months. They leave the nest aged 4-5 months.

**Notes:** Group recognises members by scent. In cold weather, group huddles and may become torpid. At 7–10 months, young leave their group to find new ranges. May live in garden nest boxes.

**Status:** Secure. Common in suitable open forests.

**Similar species:** Leadbeater's Possum lives in limited habitat and lacks membranes.

**HABITAT**
COASTAL
FORESTS

**FOOD**
SAP, NECTAR,
INSECTS

# Greater Glider

*Petauroides volans (= flying glider-like animal)*

**Length:** HB 35–45 cm
T 45–60 cm

**Weight:** 0.9-1.7 kg

**Identification:** Cat-sized glider, grey to brown above and whitish below. Short snout and large ears. Long, furry tail is not prehensile. Gliding membrane extends only to elbow.

**Where found:** Eucalypt forests and woodlands in eastern mainland Australia.

**Habits:** Feeds on eucalypt leaves. Active at night; rests in tree hollows during the day. An agile climber with two opposing toes on each front paw. Breeds from March to June. Female carries one young in pouch for 3 to 4 months.

**Notes:** Can glide up to 100 m. Defines territory by scent rather than voice.

**Status:** Vulnerable; needs undisturbed habitats with large, old trees.

**Similar species:** Yellow-bellied Glider has shorter body and longer tail.

**HABITAT**
EASTERN
WOODLANDS

**FOOD**
EUCALYPT
LEAVES

# Striped Possum

*Dactylopsila trivirgata* (= three-striped naked-finger)

**Length:** HB 25–27 cm; T 31–34 cm

**Weight:** 250–530 g

**Identification:** Small-cat-sized, slender, black and white striped possum with long, slender fourth finger. It has a strong, sweet odour.

**Where found:** Rainforests and woodlands from Iron Range south to Townsville, Qld.

**Habits:** Active at night. It is a fast, agile climber, which leaps boldly between trees. Uses its sharp teeth to pull away bark, then pokes grubs or other insects out with its tongue, or hooks them out with its long fourth finger. Sleeps during day in a hollow lined with leaves. The female has 2 young.

**Notes:** Noisy when searching for food. Fighting or mating animals shriek and gurgle.

**Status:** Probably secure. Its limited habitat needs protection.

**Similar species:** No other tree-dwelling mammal has bold stripes.

**HABITAT** RAINFOREST, NORTH QLD

**FOOD** INSECTS & SMALL LIFE

# Honey-possum

*Tarsipes rostratus* (= long-nosed tarsier*-foot)

**Length:** HB 4–9.4 cm; T 4.5–11 cm

**Weight:** 7–12 g

**Identification:** Mouse-sized, long-snouted marsupial with long prehensile tail. Eyes on top of head. Fingers and toes have broad tips and nails, not claws. Grey-brown above, with darker stripe down back.

**Where found:** Coastal heaths of southwestern WA.

**Habits:** Feeds on nectar and pollen, using long, brush-tipped tongue. Sleeps during the day in an old bird nest or hollow grasstree stem. Becomes torpid in cold weather. 2–3 young carried in pouch for 2 months, fed in nest for 2 weeks. Embryos in reserve in female's body may develop after young have been weaned.

**Notes:** Has fewer teeth than other marsupials. Depends on banksias, grevilleas, etc., for food. Acts as pollinator.

M & I MORCOMBE

**Status:** Survives where habitat is preserved.

**Similar species:** The Western Pygmy-possum has a much shorter muzzle, shorter, fatter tail, larger ears and softer fur.

\* Tarsiers, like humans, have nails rather than claws.

**HABITAT** COASTAL HEATH, WA

**FOOD** NECTAR & POLLEN

# Musky Rat-kangaroo

*Hypsiprymnodon moschatus* (= musky* animal with teeth like a potoroo)

STANLEY BREEDEN

**Length:** HB 23 cm; T ♀ 14 cm

**Weight:** ♀ 510 ♂ 530 g

**Identification:** Large-rat-sized marsupial with long scaly tail. Only kangaroo relative to have 5 toes. Sits up, holds food in paws. Moves in bounds. Grey head, brown body.

**Where found:** Rainforests of North Qld.

**Habits:** Generally solitary. Feeds in morning and late afternoon on seeds, nuts, fungi and insects. Sleeps at night in a nest on the forest floor. 2 young are carried in the pouch for 5 months, then fed in a nest.

**Notes:** Smallest of the kangaroo group, but it is like a possum in having a "big toe", a simple stomach (so it cannot digest grass) and in birthing twins. It hides seeds in the leaf litter, then eats them later.

**Status:** Probably secure. Needs rainforest areas for survival.

**Similar species:** None.

* Musk is a strong animal scent.

**HABITAT** RAINFOREST, NORTH QLD

**FOOD** SEEDS & INSECTS

# Long-nosed (Gilbert's) Potoroo

*Potorous tridactylus* (= three-toed potoroo)

**Length:** HB ♀ 34 ♂ 38 cm; T 23 cm

**Weight:** ♀ 1020 ♂ 1180 g

**Identification:** Fat-cat-sized marsupial with short feet and grasping paws. Bare skin stretches from its nose up a long snout. Moves like a little kangaroo. Grey-brown fur.

**Where found:** Scattered forests and heaths with thick ground cover and sandy soils, in coastal southeastern Aust. and Tas. One recent record in southwestern WA.

**Habits:** Feeds from dusk, digging small holes for roots, fungi and insects. Stays in or near cover. One young, carried in the pouch for 4 months.

**Notes:** Described by Governor Phillip in 1789. It has disappeared as its habitat has been cleared. Not seen in WA for over 100 years until rediscovered at Two Peoples Bay in 1994.

**Status:** Probably secure, in disappearing suitable habitat.

**Similar species:** Endangered Long-footed Potoroo, found in small areas in northeastern Vic. and southeastern NSW, is larger and has longer hindfeet.

JIRI LOCHMAN

**HABITAT**
FORESTS
& HEATHS

**FOOD**
ROOTS
& FUNGI

# Red-legged Pademelon

*Thylogale stigmatica* (= pouched-weasel with tattoos*)

**Length:** HB ♀ 46 ♂ 49 cm; T ♀ 36 ♂ 44 cm

**Weight:** ♀ 4 ♂ 5 kg

**Identification:** Small-dog-sized, stocky wallaby with short, stiff tail. Grey-brown above, cream below, with reddish cheeks, arms, hindlegs.

**Where found:** Coastal eastern Aust., from Cape York to Sydney, NSW, in dense eucalypt forest and in rainforest.

**Habits:** Feeds on leaves and fallen fruits in forest during day, grass on edges at night. Rarely grazes more than 70 m from forest edge, moving rapidly along runways.

**Notes:** Rests with tail forward under body. Warning alarm thump made with hindfeet. Joey[G] carried in pouch for 28 weeks, weaned 9 weeks later.

**Status:** Secure in limited habitat.

**Similar species:** Red-necked Pademelon has reddish fur on neck, but not on hindlegs.

* This refers to faint dotted markings on neck and hip.

**HABITAT** FOREST, RAINFOREST

**FOOD** LEAVES & GRASS

# Quokka

*Setonix brachyurus* (= bristle-footed short-tail)

**Length:** HB ♀ 47 ♂ 49 cm;
T ♀ 26.5 ♂ 29 cm

**Weight:** ♀ 2.9 ♂ 3.6 kg

**Identification:** Large-cat-sized, hopping marsupial with short ears, short, stiff tail.

**Where found:** On Rottnest Is., off WA, and in wetter parts of southwestern WA.

**Habits:** Eats leaves rather than grass. Rottnest Is. has drought in summer and local Quokkas are helped by human feeding. One joey stays in the pouch about 5 months and is weaned 2 months later. A female may carry an embryo, which continues development after her joey is weaned.

**Notes:** Once common on southwestern mainland. Second Australian marsupial to be noted by European (Willem de Vlamingh, in 1696, thought it was a big rat).

**Status:** Vulnerable. Rarely seen on mainland.

**Similar species:** On mainland, rare Brush-tailed Bettong is larger and yellowish grey. It has a longer tail with a black crest of hair.

**HABITAT**
HEATHS &
FORESTS

**FOOD**
LEAVES &
HERBS

# Yellow-footed Rock-wallaby

*Petrogale xanthopus* (= yellow-footed rock-weasel)

**Length:** HB 48–65 cm; T 57–70 cm

**Weight:** 6–11 kg

**Identification:** A colourful wallaby which hops across rocks. Grey-fawn above, white below, white stripe on cheek, side and hip. Ears, arms, hindlegs and feet are orange to yellow, tail is ringed with orange and dark brown.

**Where found:** Flinders Ranges, SA; Adavale Basin, Qld.

**Habits:** Active at night during summer, during day and night in winter. Lives in colonies of up to 100 in dry, rocky country, sometimes near water. Eats grass and leaves. Young in pouch for 6–7 months.

**Notes:** Has disappeared from former range since European settlement. Once it was heavily hunted for its skin. Today, it has to compete with feral goats and rabbits for food and drought may kill off 60% of the animals in an area.

**Status:** Vulnerable, though common in limited habitat.

**Similar species:** None.

**HABITAT** ROCKY COUNTRY

**FOOD** GRASS & LEAVES

Brush-tailed Rock-wallaby

Black-footed Rock-wallaby

Nabarlek

Monjon (Warabi)

IAN MORRIS

43

# Pretty-face Wallaby

*Macropus parryi* (= Parry's great-foot)

**Length:** HB ♀ up to 75.5 ♂ up to 92 cm; T 78–94 cm

**Weight:** 11–16 kg

**Identification:** Medium-sized wallaby with long, slender tail, grey or brownish-grey above, white below. Dark brown forehead, base of ears. White stripe on upper lip, white stripe on hip and brown stripe down neck to shoulder.

**Where found:** Coastal eastern Aust. from Cooktown, Qld, to northern NSW, in areas with trees and grass.

**Habits:** Feeds during day on grass. Lives in groups of up to 50, each made up of smaller groups of 10 or less. Dominant[G] male mates with female. Joey carried in pouch for 37 weeks, then suckled another 9 months. Reserve embryo develops when pouch vacant.

**Notes:** When alarmed, thumps ground with hindfeet.

**Status:** Secure. Common.

**Similar species:** Black-striped Wallaby has dark back stripe.

**HABITAT** WOODLAND, FOREST

**FOOD** GRASSES

# Agile Wallaby

*Macropus agilis* (= agile great-foot)

IAN MORRIS

**Length:** HB ♀ 65 ♂ 80 cm; T ♀ 74 ♂ 77 cm

**Weight:** ♀ 11 ♂ 19 kg

**Identification:** Large wallaby, brown above, whitish below. Light stripe on thigh, dark stripe up forehead, pale stripe on cheek. Hops with body almost upright, tail held straight out behind.

**Where found:** Grasslands across northern Aust. and down northeastern Qld coast.

**Habits:** Eats native grasses. Lives in groups of up to 10 which may become large mobs at feeding areas. Wary, easily alarmed. Joey stays in pouch 7–8 months, follows female until 12 months. Reserve embryo develops when pouch vacant.

**Notes:** Males much larger than females.

**Status:** Secure. Common.

**Similar species:** Several, but all far less common.

**HABITAT** GRASS LANDS

**FOOD** NATIVE GRASSES

Red-necked (Bennett's) Wallaby

Swamp Wallaby

Bridled Nailtail Wallaby

Parma Wallaby

# Red-necked (Bennett's*) Wallaby

*Macropus rufogriseus* (= red-grey great-foot)

**Length:** HB ♀ 77 ♂ 82 cm; T ♀ 72 ♂ 80 cm

**Weight:** ♀ 14 ♂ 19 kg

**Identification:** A medium-sized wallaby, grey to reddish above, with reddish-brown neck. Pale grey below. Black muzzle, paws and largest toe. White stripe on upper lip.

**Where found:** Eucalypt forests of southeastern Aust. and Tas. Grazes in open grassy areas bordering forest.

**Habits:** Solitary, but may graze in groups. Spends day in forest, feeds from late afternoon. Eats grasses and leaves.

**Notes:** Group splits into single animals when disturbed. Protected, but may be killed in open seasons in Qld and Tas. Joey carried in pouch for 40 weeks, then suckled for another 5–7 months. Reserve embryo stored in female develops and is born after joey leaves pouch.

**Status:** Secure. Common.

**Similar species:** Black-striped Wallaby in Qld and northern NSW has dark stripe down back and white stripe on hip.

* Name of the species in Tasmania.

**HABITAT** EUCALYPT FORESTS

**FOOD** GRASS & LEAVES

# Lumholtz's Tree-kangaroo

*Dendrolagus lumholtzi* (= Lumholtz's tree-hare)

STANLEY BREEDEN

**Identification:** Medium-sized tree-climbing kangaroo with long, non-prehensile tail, strong front and hind limbs. Brownish-black in colour, with lighter fur on lower back. Pale brown band across forehead and down each side of face.

**Where found:** In highland rainforest in a very limited area of northeastern Qld.

**Habits:** Solitary. Spends day asleep, crouched in treetop. Eats leaves and fruit, holding them in paws. Joey stays in pouch for around 33 weeks.

**Notes:** Once lived in coastal rainforests, but has retreated to higher habitat. Good climber, with strong claws, short, broad feet. Tree-kangaroos are the only kangaroos able to walk rather than hop.

**Status:** Vulnerable.

**Length:** HB ♀ 55 ♂ 59 cm; T 70 cm

**Weight:** 6–7.5 kg

**Similar species:** Bennett's Tree-kangaroo lacks pale head markings.

**HABITAT** HIGHLAND RAINFORESTS

**FOOD** LEAVES & FRUITS

# Eastern Grey Kangaroo

*Macropus giganteus* (= gigantic great-foot)

**Length:** HB ♀ 96–186 ♂ 98–230 cm; T ♀ 45–84 ♂ 43–110 cm

**Weight:** ♀ up to 66 ♂ up to 32 kg

**Identification:** Large grey or grey-brown kangaroo with paler underparts. Unlike other kangaroos, has hair on muzzle between nostrils and upper lip.

**Where found:** Scrubland, woodland and forest from inland plains to eastern coastal Aust. and northeastern Tas.

**Habits:** Rests in the shade during day, then eats grasses from late afternoon to early morning. Males are larger than females and dominant males mate with most females. Joey carried in pouch 11 months, suckles another 9 months. Reserve embryo develops when pouch vacant.

**Notes:** Has increased using water and feed provided for cattle and sheep.

**Status:** Secure. Common.

**Similar species:** The Western Grey Kangaroo is browner than the Eastern Grey, and its range lies more to the west.

**HABITAT**
SCRUBLANDS
& WOODLANDS

**FOOD**
GRASSES

# Red Kangaroo

*Macropus rufus* (= red great-foot)

**Length:** HB ♀ 100 ♂ 115 cm; T ♀ 82 ♂ 88 cm

**Weight:** ♀ 26.5 ♂ 66 kg

**Identification:** Very large

kangaroo (an exceptional male may weigh up to 85 kg). Red (male) or blue-grey or reddish (female) above, whitish below. Black and white patches at sides of muzzle, white stripe from mouth to ear. Naked area between nostril and lip.

**Where found:** Inland plains and woodlands, where water and green feed are available.

**Habits:** Rests during heat of day, feeds from dusk.

**Notes:** In drought, breeding activity in both males and females slows and pouch young may die. After rain, when green feed is available, breeding is successful. Each group led by a dominant male.

**Status:** Secure. Has probably increased in numbers since European settlement. Like Eastern Grey Kangaroo, when numbers build up may be harvested for meat and skins.

**Similar species:** None.

**HABITAT** INLAND PLAINS

**FOOD** GRASSES

# Common Wallaroo (Euro)

*Macropus robustus* (= strong great-foot)

**Length:** HB ♀ 134 ♂ 156 cm; T: ♀ 64 ♂ 73 cm

**Weight:** ♀ 15.5 ♂ 26.5 kg

**Identification:** Large kangaroo usually found in rocky hill country. Dark grey or brown above, paler below. Fur coarse and sometimes shaggy. Area between nostril and lip is naked.

**Where found:** Drier areas of Aust., except for southwest and southeast. Not in Tas.

**Habits:** Solitary, on rocky hillslopes with grazing nearby. Shelters under ledges during day, eats grasses and shrubs at night. Can survive without drinking frequently.

**Notes:** Large male may be twice female weight. Called different names in east and west. Shaggy, dark grey Eastern Wallaroo lives on eastern and western slopes of Great Dividing Range. Shorter-haired, reddish Euro takes its

place across to the west coast.

**Status:** Secure. Common.

**Similar species:** Antilopine Wallaroo, more often seen on flatter country in far northern Australia, sometimes feeds with Euros near water.

**HABITAT** ROCKY HILL SLOPES

**FOOD** GRASSES & SHRUBS

# ❤ Spectacled Flying-fox

*Pteropus conspicillatus* (= spectacled wing-foot)

**Identification:** Large megabat[G] with black body and wings, yellowish fur around eyes and down muzzle, neck ruff of yellow hair. Male ruff may be reddish from scented body fluid used in grooming.

**Where found:** Camps and feeds in or near rainforest in northeastern Qld.

**Habits:** Spends day in camp, flies out after dusk to feed on fruit, mainly in rainforest. One young one is carried by its mother while she feeds for 5 months.

**Notes:** Feeds on rainforest fruits. Carries fruit away to feed, or passes seeds through gut, so helps rainforest regeneration.

**Status:** Vulnerable. Disappears as rainforest cleared.

**Length:** HB 22–24 cm

**Weight:** ♀ 500–650 g; ♂ 580–850 g

**Similar species:** Black and Grey-headed Flying-foxes lack very pale eye-rings.

**HABITAT**
NE QLD
RAINFOREST

**FOOD**
RAINFOREST
FRUITS

# Ghost Bat

*Macroderma gigas* (= giant large-skin)

**Length:** HB 10–13 cm

**Weight:** 140–165 g

**Identification:** Large microbat[G] with large eyes, large ears joined at their bases and a simple noseleaf[G]. Fur grey above, paler below.

**Where found:** Groups survive in scattered locations across northern Aust. Roosts in caves, mine shafts, crevices.

**Habits:** At night swoops on small animals, including bats, holds them in its wings, bites and kills them, then carries them to a perch to be eaten. May use echolocation[G]. One young born Sept–Nov.

**Notes:** Has decreased in numbers in last 200 years.

**Status:** Rare and endangered.

**Similar species:** None.

**HABITAT**
ROOSTS IN CAVES

**FOOD**
SMALL ANIMALS

# Bush Rat

*Rattus fuscipes* (= dusky-footed rat)

**Length:** HB 11–21 cm; T 10–19 cm

**Weight:** 40–225 g

**Identification:** Rat with pink, rounded ears and tail shorter than head and body.

**Where found:** In coastal forests, woodland and scrub with dense undergrowth in southwest, southeast and northeast Aust.

**Habits:** Prefers thick undergrowth. Eats grass-stems and leaves, fungi and insects.

**Notes:** Females are much smaller than males. Five young in a litter; are independent of their mother at 4–5 weeks. Only the season's young survive winter to breed in springtime. In High Country of southeastern NSW and northeastern Vic., lives in runways under snow in winter.

**Status:** Secure. Common in undisturbed habitat, but suffers when this is logged or burned. Repopulates after rain falls.

**Similar species:** Introduced Black Rat has longer tail and lives around human settlement.

JIRI LOCHMAN

| HABITAT DENSE UNDERGROWTH | FOOD GRASS & FUNGI |
| --- | --- |

# Spinifex Hopping-mouse

*Notomys alexis* (= Alexandria Downs southern mouse)

**Length:** HB 10 cm; T 14 cm

**Weight:** 27–45 g

**Identification:** A rat-sized, hopping mouse, with large ears, long hindfeet and a very long, brush-tipped tail. Has a pouch under the throat. Pale brown above, white below.

**Where found:** Amongst spinifex on sand dunes and sandy flats in northwestern and central Aust.

**Habits:** Shelters from heat in below-ground nest chamber connected by shafts to surface. Eats seeds, roots and insects.

**Notes:** Hopping-mice use all four limbs when moving slowly, rise to hindlimbs to move at speed. 3–4 young are left in nest while female looks for food. Either female or male may retrieve a young one which wanders from the nest.

**Status:** Rare in dry conditions, breeds up after rainfall.

**Similar species:** Short-tailed Hopping Mouse (in the same habitat) is probably extinct.

M & I MORCOMBE

**HABITAT** ARID SAND COUNTRY

**FOOD** SEEDS & INSECTS

# Introduced mammals

These and many other kinds of mammals have escaped or been released into the wild. They compete with native animals for food and homes. Some also prey on wildlife.

Fox

Cat

Pig

Goat

Camel

56

# Dingo

*Canis lupus* (= dog-wolf)

**Length:** HB 86–122 cm; T 26–38 cm

**Weight:** 9.6–24 kg

**Identification:** Medium-sized dog, usually yellowish-ginger but sometimes black-and-tan or white. Usually white markings on chest, tail tip and paws. Pricked ears and bushy tail.

**Where found:** All Aust. except for Tas.

**Habits:** Lives in packs which may meet at intervals or stay together. Breed once a year. Only dominant male and female may breed, while others help rear pups. Takes whatever prey is common at the time, from insects to large mammals such as kangaroos.

**Notes:** Developed from Indian Wolf around 6000 years ago. Brought to Australia less than 4000 years ago by seafarers. Hunting by humans does not balance increase allowed by bores, dams and rabbits.

**Status:** Secure. Common.

**Similar species:** Some breeds of domestic dog. Hybrids between Dingo and domestic dog are increasing.

**HABITAT** NEAR FOOD & SHELTER

**FOOD** ANIMALS, ALL SIZES

# Bottlenosed Dolphin

*Tursiops truncatus* (= short-faced dolphin)

**Length:** 340–390 cm

**Weight:** 150–650 kg

**Identification:** Large, streamlined marine mammal with beaky snout, rounded forehead, backward-pointing dorsal[G] fin. Grey above, paler grey sides, off-white below.

**Where found:** In coastal or offshore waters anywhere around Aust. and Tas.

**Habits:** Usually in small groups. Often rides bow-waves of boats. Dives last up to 4 minutes, shows forehead but not beak when surfacing.

**Notes:** Eats fish, squid and other marine animals. Inquisitive and active; sometimes visits beaches.

**Status:** Probably secure.

**Similar species:** Dugong (p. 53).

**HABITAT**
COASTS &
SEAS

**FOOD**
FISH &
MARINE LIFE

# Australian Sea-lion

*Neophoca cinerea* (= ash-coloured new-seal)

**Length:** HBT ♀ 160 ♂ 210 cm

**Weight:** ♀ 80 ♂ 300 kg

**Identification:** Seal with blunt snout and small rolled ears; on land, props itself upright on front flippers. Male dark with white crown and nape; female ash-grey above, cream below.

**Where found:** On offshore islands from the Abrolhos, WA, to Kangaroo Island, SA.

**Habits:** Swims using front flippers. Feeds at sea on squids and other marine creatures. Comes ashore on sandy beaches but breeds on rocky beaches, from Oct–Jan.

**Notes:** Only seal or sea-lion found exclusively in Aust. Hunted to near-extinction by sealers; absent from Bass Strait. Aggressive while breeding.

**Status:** Rare and vulnerable. There are only 3000–5000 Australian Sea-lions.

**Similar species:** Australian Fur-seal has dense underfur.

**HABITAT** SEA & SEASHORE

**FOOD** MARINE ANIMALS

# Humpback Whale

*Megaptera novaeangliae* (= New England great-wings)

**Length:** HBT 15 m

**Weight:** 25–45 tonnes

**Identification:** Large whale with massive head bearing callosities[G] on top and on lower jaw. 14–24 grooves on throat. Flippers are one-third as long as body. Hump in front of dorsal fin. Black above, mainly white below.

**Where found:** In winter, migrate from Antarctic waters up coasts of Australia to breed in warmer sub-tropical waters. Return in springtime.

**Habits:** Feeds on krill[G], filtered from Antarctic seas by baleen[G] in mouth. Does not feed while migrating. Males compete aggressively for right to mate with females.

**Notes:** Humpback Whales "sing" by shifting air around spaces in their bodies. All whales in an area sing the same song, which changes throughout the season.

**Status:** Since end of whaling, numbers have increased.

**Similar species:** Southern Right Whale has blunt-ended flippers, large, lumpy, white callosities on head.

**HABITAT**
SEAS

**FOOD**
KRILL

# Dugong

*Dugong dugon* (= Dugong)

**Length:** HBT ♀ 219 ♂ 223 cm

**Weight:** 420 kg

**Identification:** Large, blunt-muzzled sea mammal with flippers and horizontal tail flukes[G]. Grey to brown above, paler below.

**Where found:** In shallow, calm, warm, sub-tropical and tropical coastal waters from Shark Bay, WA, around north of Aust. to Moreton Bay, Qld.

**Habits:** Lives in herds; feeds on seagrasses. Female breeds after reaching 9 years of age. Calf rides just above her back.

**Notes:** Dense bones keep it on the bottom while using broad upper lip to manipulate seagrasses into the mouth.

**Status:** Vulnerable to habitat alteration, hunting, netting.

**Similar species:** Bottlenosed Dolphin has a pointed snout, one blowhole on top of the head and a dorsal fin.

GEOFF TAYLOR

**HABITAT**
SHALLOW
SEAS

**FOOD**
SEA-
GRASSES

# Birds

An animal is a bird if it:

- has a backbone and skull
- is warm-blooded and has a four-chambered heart
- breathes air and has lungs
- has feathers
- has one pair of legs and one pair of wings or flippers
- has a bill (beak)
- lays hard-shelled eggs

## Where and when

The best time to see and hear birds is from dawn to early morning, with late afternoon to dusk as a second choice. Few birds are active in the middle of the day or in wet or windy weather.

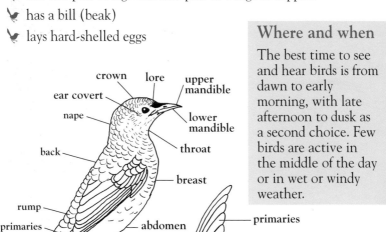

# Bird groups

Often birds are divided into two simple groups based on the structure of their feet and voice boxes.

*Passerines* are known as perching or song birds. They have a foot with three forward-pointing toes and one non-reversible toe that points backwards. They have a well-developed voice box and communicate with song. Passerines build complex nests.

| | |
|---|---|
| Passerines | Fairy-wrens, finches, robins, honeyeaters |

*Non-passerines* are all other groups of birds including:

| | |
|---|---|
| Struthioniformes | Emu, cassowary |
| Podicipediformes | grebes |
| Sphenisciformes | penguins |
| Pelecaniformes | pelicans, cormorants |
| Ardeiformes | storks, ibis, egrets |
| Anseriformes | ducks, geese, swans |
| Accipitriformes | eagles, hawks |
| Galliformes | Malleefowl, brush-turkey |
| Gruiformes | cranes, swamphens, bustards |
| Charadriiformes | gulls, curlews, jacanas |
| Columbiformes | pigeons, doves |
| Psittaciformes | parrots, cockatoos, lorikeets |
| Cuculiformes | cuckoos, coucals |
| Strigiformes | owls, boobooks |
| Caprimulgiformes | frogmouths, nightjars |
| Coraciiformes | kingfishers, kookaburras |

# Eastern Yellow Robin

*Eopsaltria australis* (= southern dawn-harper)

**Length:** 14–15 cm

**Identification:** Small, plump bird with grey upperparts, yellow rump, white chin, yellow underparts. White wingbar shows in flight.

**Call:** Loud whistle *tewp-tewp* before dawn; soft piping.

**Where found:** Forests and woodlands with bushy undergrowth, in eastern Australia.

**Habits:** Alone, in pairs, or in small parties, sometimes with other small birds. Hunts insects by perching, watching, then pouncing. May cling sideways to tree trunk.

**Nesting:** Mated pair holds territory. Female builds cup nest of bark and grass bound by cobwebs, decorates outside with lichens, in tree fork. Male feeds her while she incubates 2–3 spotted eggs for 15–16 days. Both parents, plus helpers from previous broods, feed young.

**Notes:** A quiet and charming bird, which may become tame in a garden, or around a picnic place.

**Status:** Common.

**Similar species:** Western Yellow Robin in southwestern WA.

RAOUL SLATER

HABITAT
WOODLANDS
& FORESTS

FOOD
INSECTS &
SMALL LIFE

# Golden Whistler

*Pachycephala pectoralis* (= breasted thick-head)

**Length:** 16–17 cm

**Identification:** Small, large-headed bird which sits upright, moves slowly when feeding. Male has black head and collar, white throat, golden nape and breast, green upperparts. Female is grey-brown, with white throat.

**Call:** Rich *wh-wh-wh-you wit*, with whipcrack ending.

**Where found:** Forests of southern and eastern Australia and southwestern WA.

GRAEME CHAPMAN

**Habits:** Alone or in pairs, hops through trees, flies around foliage, eating insects.

**Nesting:** Male and female both sing, defend territory, build a cup nest of plant stems, leaves held together with cobweb in a fork. Take turns to incubate 2 spotted eggs for 14–17 days. Both feed young.

**Notes:** A loud noise may start whistlers singing their beautiful, rich notes. In winter, mountain and southern birds may move to warmer areas.

**Status:** Common.

**Similar species:** Mangrove Golden Whistler only in northern mangroves. Rufous Whistler has red-brown breast.

**HABITAT** WOODLANDS & FORESTS

**FOOD** INSECTS & SMALL LIFE

# Eastern Spinebill

*Acanthorhynchus tenuirostris (= narrow-beaked spine-bill)*

**Length:** 13–16 cm

**Identification:** A tiny honeyeater with long, slender bill. Male has black head, curved neck stripe, cinnamon bib, nape and abdomen. Female duller with grey-brown crown.

**Call:** short, sharp piping or soft chee-chee-chee.

**Where found:** Forest and woodland understorey, heath and gardens in eastern Australia and Tasmania.

**Habits:** Hovers over flowers to feed on nectar; also eats insects. Defends feeding and nesting sites. Inquisitive.

**Nesting:** Pairs build cup of bark and grass bound with cobwebs in shrub or low branches. Male and female incubate 2 to 3 blotched, buff to pinkish eggs.

**Notes:** Migrates locally in SE Aust.; sedentary elsewhere.

**Status:** Common in range.

**Similar species:** Tawny-crowned Honeyeater has white throat; Crescent Honeyeater has yellow wing panel.

**HABITAT** WOODLANDS & GARDENS

**FOOD** INSECTS & NECTAR

# Splendid Fairy-wren

*Malurus splendens* (= shining soft-tailed bird)

**Length:** 12–14 cm

**Identification:** Tiny, plump bird with long, cocked tail. Adult male pale blue crown, cheek patches and upper back, black mask and collar; back black and blue, wings and underparts blue. Female and young male are brown.

**Call:** Trilling *treee*; loud, rich, warbling song.

**Where found:** Open forest and woodland in central and southwestern Aust.

**Habits:** Family group consists of pair plus helpers, usually young males from past broods. Feeds on insects and other small creatures.

**Nesting:** Female builds domed nest of grass and bark in bush, incubates 3–4 spotted eggs for first part of 13–15 days. Helpers aid later incubation, then assist in feeding chicks.

**Notes:** High mortality from cats and fire, in spite of good

PETER SLATER

family care of chicks. Intruder male may invade territory carrying a flower, then be accepted by a female as mate.

**Status:** Common.

**Similar species:** Superb Fairy-wren in southeastern Australia has black back and breast, white underparts.

**HABITAT**
OPEN
WOODLANDS

**FOOD**
SMALL
LIFE

# Spotted Pardalote

*Pardalotus punctatus* (= spotted spotted-bird)

RAOUL SLATER

**Length:** 90–100 mm

**Identification:** Tiny, short-tailed, stubby-beaked bird which feeds in treetops. Black crown, wings and tail, spotted with white; yellow to red back and rump, yellow undertail. Female paler than male.

**Call:** High *sleep-baby*.

**Where found:** Wetter forests in eastern, southeastern and southwestern Australia.

**Habits:** Moves fast through leaves of eucalypts feeding on lerps and other insects. Out of breeding season feeds in flocks, which may move to warmer feeding grounds in winter.

**Nesting:** A pair digs a nest tunnel in an earth bank, wall, or mound of garden soil. In a nest chamber lined with bark and grass, they take turns to incubate 3–6 white eggs for 14 days, then feed the chicks.

**Notes:** Pardalotes are only found in Australia and make their living in the crowns of eucalypts. The Forty-spotted Pardalote, found only in southeastern Tasmania, is an endangered species.

**Status:** Common.

**Similar species:** Striated Pardalote is found all over Australia. It has white streaks on its head, but no spots.

 **HABITAT**
EUCALYPT
FORESTS

 **FOOD**
TREETOP
INSECTS

# Zebra Finch

*Taeniopygia guttata* (= spotted banded-rump)

**Length:** 10 cm

**Identification:** Tiny red-billed finch with black and white on face, grey upperparts, chestnut cheek patches, black and white rump, white spots on red flanks.

**Call:** Nasal *tang*.

**Where found:** All over Australia except Cape York Peninsula, extreme southwest and southeastern Tas.

**Habits:** Found where there is grass seed to eat, bushes to nest in, water to drink. Can survive dry conditions. Lives in flocks, roosts in special grass nests.

**Nesting:** Breeds whenever rain has fallen and seed is plentiful. Nest is a woven ball of grass with a side tunnel entrance. The male fetches grass, while the female builds. Both birds incubate the 4–5 white eggs for 12–14 days, then both feed the young.

**Notes:** One of the world's best-known cage birds, with white and other colour varieties.

**Status:** Common.

**Similar species:** None.

RAOUL SLATER

**HABITAT** GRASS-LANDS

**FOOD** GRASS SEEDS

# Willy Wagtail

*Rhipidura leucophrys* (= white-browed fan-tail)

**Length:** 19–21 cm

**Identification:** Small bird with black upperparts and throat, white underparts and eyebrow. Long tail is fanned and wagged from side to side.

**Call:** Rattling in aggression; song *sweet-pretty-creature* often given on moonlight night.

**Where found:** Anywhere on mainland and northern Tas. Farms, suburbs.

**Habits:** Perches, then flies to catch insects; hops around taking prey on open ground.

**Nesting:** May nest near human dwelling. Male and female build cup of bark and grass, stuck together with cobwebs, on branch. Both incubate 2–4 spotted eggs for 14 days, then feed the chicks.

**Notes:** Willy Wagtail shows dominance by flashing white eyebrow. Uses sheep, cattle as perches. Noisy and aggressive towards hawks, snakes, cats.

**Status:** Common.

**Similar species:** Restless Flycatcher has a white throat, makes scissor-grinding call, hovers over grass looking for insects.

RAOUL SLATER

 **HABITAT** SUBURBS & FARMLANDS

 **FOOD** INSECTS

# Australian Magpie

*Gymnorhina tibicen* (= flute-playing naked-nose)

**Length:** 38–44 cm

**Identification:** Medium-sized, strong-legged bird with black head and underparts, white nape, white on wing. Both sexes have black backs over most of eastern and northern Australia; male has white back, female ashy-grey back in Vic., Tas., southwest of WA.

**Call:** Loud, sweet song; softer whisper-song includes mimicry of other birds.

**Where found:** Open country with trees, all over Australia. Farms, suburbs, cities.

**Habits:** A group of up to 24 birds defends territory, feeds on ground on insects and other small animals. Dominant male mates with several females.

**Nesting:** Neighbouring groups battle with song for territory. A female build a nest of sticks in a tall tree, lays 3–5 blotched eggs, incubates 20 days and feeds young. Once out of the nest, young may be fed by others in group.

**Notes:** Nests supported by dominant male have best chance of succeeding. Young are later driven from group and form roving flocks. (If magpies defending nests become aggressive, wear a hat, or take another route.)

**Status:** Common.

**Similar species:** None.

**HABITAT**
SUBURBS &
FARMLANDS

**FOOD**
INSECTS,
SMALL LIFE

# Superb Lyrebird

*Menura novaehollandiae* (= mighty-tailed Australian bird)

**Length:** ♂ 80–100 cm (of which tail is 50–60 cm)

**Identification:** Large, brown ground-bird. Male has long filmy tail, thrown over back when he displays; female has shorter, plainer tail.

**Call:** Male is master of song and mimicry.

**Where found:** Coastal wet forests of southeastern Australia; introduced to Tas.

**Habits:** Scratches forest floor for small animals. Male claims territory by singing and dancing on earthen display mounds; females come to the mound to mate.

**Nesting:** Female builds a domed nest of sticks, incubates 1 blotched egg for up to 50 days, then cares for young.

**Notes:** Depends on wet forest habitat for survival.

**Status:** May be endangered.

**Similar species:** Albert's Lyrebird, smaller and with shorter tail, in northeastern NSW and southeastern Qld.

**HABITAT**
WET
FORESTS

**FOOD**
FOREST
FLOOR ANIMALS

# Satin Bowerbird

*Ptilinorhynchus violaceus* (= blue feather-bill)

RAOUL SLATER

**Length:** 28–34 cm

**Identification:** Medium-sized blue-black bird with mauve eyes (male), or with green upperparts, creamy underparts marked with spots on throat, scallops on breast and belly (female and young male).

**Call:** Near bower, male chatters, buzzes, creaks, and mimics other birds and sounds.

**Where found:** Mountain and coastal forests in eastern Australia, from Atherton Tableland, Qld, to Otway Ranges, Victoria.

**Habits:** Flocks in autumn and winter, seeking fruit and seeds. In spring, males return to their bowers, which are avenues of sticks built in forest clearings. They decorate these with blue objects, then dance and sing to attract females.

**Nesting:** Female mates with male with finest bower, then builds saucer of twigs in tree, incubates 2–3 spotted and blotched eggs for 21–22 days, then raises young by herself.

**Notes:** Males do not get full blue plumage until they are 6 or 7 years old. Until then they practise bower-building. Bower may be painted with plant juice, charcoal, saliva.

**Status:** Common in suitable habitat.

**Similar species:** None.

**HABITAT** COASTAL RAINFORESTS

**FOOD** FRUITS, SEEDS & INSECTS

# Laughing Kookaburra

*Dacelo novaeguineae* (= New Guinea kingfisher)

**Length:** 40–45 cm

**Identification:** Medium-sized kingfisher with dark mask, dark eye, brown upperparts, white collar and underparts. Pale blue on wing, brown tail is barred black. In flight, shows white band across wing.

**Call:** Chuckling; loud "laughing" made by group to claim territory.

**Where found:** Woodland and open forest in northeastern, eastern and southeastern Australia; introduced to southwestern WA.

**Habits:** Alone or in pairs, sitting on wire or branch, watching for insects, frogs, reptiles. Prey battered on perch, then swallowed.

**Nesting:** In a tree hollow or hole in termite mound. 1–4 white eggs incubated for 24 days by female and helpers, who also feed chicks.

**Notes:** Unmated young birds, up to 4 years of age, help their parents raise new chicks.

**Status:** Common.

**Similar species:** Blue-winged Kookaburra, across northern Australia, has white, streaked head, pale eye, more blue on wing. Shrieking call.

**HABITAT**
WOODLANDS
& FORESTS

**FOOD**
SMALL
ANIMALS

# Sacred Kingfisher

*Todirhamphus sancta* (= sacred tody-bill*)

RAOUL SLATER

**Length:** 19–23 cm

**Identification:** Small kingfisher with black mask, buff spot in front of eye, white collar, blue-green upperparts, blue edge to wings, blue tail; pale buff underparts.

**Call:** Repeated *kik-kik-kik*.

**Where found:** All over Australia, except for driest parts, in spring and summer. Spends period March to October in islands to the north of Australia.

**Habits:** Usually alone, sitting on wire or branch, watching for insects, frogs or reptiles. May catch tadpoles, small fish in shallow water.

**Nesting:** Pair digs tunnel in termite nest, tree limb or earth bank. Take turns to incubate 3–6 white eggs for 16–17 days, then both feed chicks.

**Notes:** May be killed by cats when pouncing on ground prey in gardens.

**Status:** Common.

**Similar species:** Forest Kingfisher has white patch in wing; Red-backed Kingfisher has head streaked white.

* Todies are West Indian birds.

**HABITAT** ANYWHERE EXCEPT DESERT

**FOOD** SMALL ANIMALS

# Rainbow Bee-eater

*Merops ornatus* (= ornate bee-eater)

**Length:** 21–24 cm

**Identification:** Dainty, slender-winged, green-gold bird with fine down-curving bill, black mask, black throat, gold on head and under wings, two long central tail feathers.

**Call:** Repeated *prrrp-prrrp*, often in flight.

**Where found:** Open country with trees and bushes to perch on, soil or earth banks for nesting, anywhere in Australia except Tasmania.

**Habits:** Usually with other bee-eaters, sitting on wires or branches, darting out to take dragonflies, wasps or other insects on wing.

**Nesting:** Nest in 1 m tunnel dug into flat, sandy ground or earth bank. Mated pair may be

RAOUL SLATER

helped by young, unmated birds. Four to five white eggs are incubated for 21–25 days. Young leave nest at 1 month.

**Notes:** Breeds in Australia; most spend winter in islands to Australia's north. Sometimes roosts in large groups.

**Status:** Common in summer.

**Similar species:** Kingfishers have straight, stout bills.

**HABITAT** OPEN COUNTRY

**FOOD** FLYING INSECTS

# Tawny Frogmouth

*Podargus strigoides* (= trap-footed owl-like bird)

**Length:** 35–53 cm

**Identification:** Medium-sized night-bird, whose mottled and streaked grey, brown, black and white feathers and upright posture camouflage[G] it as a broken-off branch. Wide bill, weak legs, small feet.

**Call:** Soft, repeated, far-carrying *oom-oom-oom*.

**Where found:** All over Australia.

**Habits:** Often seen in a pair, or family group. Roosts during day, freezing and sky-pointing bill if disturbed. Hunts after dark, perching then flying down to snap up insects, frogs and other small animals with wide, sharp-edged bill.

**Nesting:** Male and female mate for life. They build a flimsy stick nest in a tree fork, incubate 1–3 white eggs for 28–32 days, then both feed the young.

**Notes:** Garden insecticides eaten with prey may be stored in body fat. When fat is used in cold weather, poisons cause convulsions, death.

**Status:** Common.

**Similar species:** Marbled and Papuan Frogmouths are seldom-seen rainforest species.

PETER SLATER

**HABITAT**
ANYWHERE
WITH TREES

**FOOD**
SMALL
ANIMALS

# 🦉 Barn Owl

*Tyto alba* (= white owl)

**Length:** 30–40 cm

**Identification:** Medium-sized, pale-coloured owl, with heart-shaped white facial disc around dark eyes, pale bill and long, bare legs. White underparts, grey-gold upperparts; wings are spotted black and white.

**Call:** Rasping hiss, like cloth ripping.

**Where found:** All over Australia, especially open woodland and plains.

**Habits:** Favourite food mice, so often seen around farm buildings. Hunts after dark, watching from perch then pouncing silently. Builds up numbers in mouse plagues, but many owls die afterwards.

**Nesting:** Breeds when food is plentiful. Nests in tree hollow or cave. Female incubates 3–7 white eggs for 33–35 days; male helps feed chicks.

**Notes:** Locates prey by sound and has keen night vision. Roosts during day in hollow, foliage or cave. Under roost are pellets of food remains.

**Status:** Common in suitable habitat, but seldom seen.

**Similar species:** Grass Owl (a rare inhabitant of grasslands) has tawny-brown back. Masked Owl is larger.

**HABITAT**
ALL OVER
AUSTRALIA

**FOOD**
SMALL
ANIMALS

# Southern Boobook

*Ninox novaeseelandiae* (= New Zealand night-bird)

**Length:** 25–35 cm

**Identification:** Small, dark-coloured owl with a circular disc around each yellow-green eye, dark bill and shortish, feathered legs. Upperparts brown with white spots, underparts streaked white, wings barred.

**Call:** Repeated *boo-book*, second note lower.

**Where found:** All over Australia.

**Habits:** Hunts for small roosting birds, insects and small mammals in hours after sunset and before sunrise.

**Nesting:** Courting pair sits side by side preening[G] each other. Nests in tree hollow. Female incubates 2–4 white eggs for about 30 days while fed by male; both parents feed young.

**Notes:** Other birds will mob roosting Boobook, which sits upright, feathers sleeked. May live in suburbs, catch moths at outdoor lights, visit bird baths.

**Status:** Common.

**Similar species:** Barking Owl larger, white blotches on upperparts, bold white streaks on underparts. Barking call.

IAN MORRIS

**HABITAT**
ALL OVER
AUSTRALIA

**FOOD**
SMALL
ANIMALS

# Shining Bronze-Cuckoo

*Chrysococcyx lucidus* (= shining golden-cuckoo)

**Length:** 17–18 cm

**Identification:** Small, plump bird with loose-looking feathers, fine bill. Shining green-bronze back, striped underparts. Flies in up-and-down pattern on slender, pointed wings.

**Call:** Male calls in repeated high, rising whistle, like someone calling a dog.

**Where found:** High rainfall coastal areas from Cape York, Qld to SA, and the southwest of WA.

**Habits:** Winters north of Australia, arrives in Australia August, breeds by January, then most migrate north again. Eats insects, including hairy caterpillars, which most birds will not touch.

**Nesting:** Male attracts female by calling. After mating, female places egg in nest of host; cuckoo hatches in 17 days, shoves out hosts' eggs or chicks, then is raised by hosts. A female may lay up to 16 eggs a season.

**Notes:** Hosts usually small birds with domed nests, e.g. fairy-wrens.

**Status:** Common, but only calling male easy to spot, after following call.

**Similar species:** Horsfield's Bronze-Cuckoo has dark spot on cheek, is paler in colour.

GRAEME CHAPMAN

| HABITAT WOODLANDS & FORESTS | FOOD CATERPILLARS, OTHER INSECTS |

# Pheasant Coucal

*Centropus phasianinus* (= spur-footed pheasant-like bird)

**Length:** 50–60 cm

**Identification:** Large, long-tailed, loose-feathered, ground-living bird which suns itself in treetop at dawn, scuttles without warning across road. In breeding season, has glossy black head, back, breast, wings barred russet, buff, black. Non-breeding head and back buff and russet.

**Call:** Repeated bubbling *oop-oop-oop*, first falling, then rising and getting faster.

**Where found:** Dense undergrowth and grasses in coastal northern and eastern Australia.

**Habits:** Hunts insects, frogs, mice and other small animals.

**Nesting:** Nest of leafy twigs and grass on platform trampled in a bush. Both parents incubate 2–5 white eggs for 15 days, then feed young. May nest again while young still being fed in area.

**Notes:** Sometimes wrongly thought to be a pheasant. Bubbling call betrays birds hunting in outer suburban gardens at dawn. Young will leave nest early if disturbed.

**Status:** Common where suitable habitat exists.

**Similar species:** None.

RAOUL SLATER

**HABITAT**
WOODLANDS
& GRASSES

**FOOD**
SMALL
ANIMALS

# Yellow-tailed Black-Cockatoo

*Calyptorhynchus funereus* (= funeral-like cover-beak)

**Length:** 58 – 65 cm

**Identification:** Large, black cockatoo with long tail and small crest. Male has brown eye, yellow cheek patch and tail panel. Female has grey eye, larger cheek patch and white bill.

**Call:** Harsh screech; drawn out *whee-la*.

**Where found:** Rainforest, eucalypt forest and woodland, heath, pine plantations in SE Australia.

**Habits:** Eats pine, banksia and hakea seeds, also wood grubs. Found in pairs or small groups.

**Nesting:** Pair nest in high tree hollows. Female incubates two white eggs; only one offspring survives.

**Notes:** Flight is buoyant with slow wing beats. Chicks remain dependent until next breeding season.

**Status:** Vulnerable to habitat clearance.

**Similar species:** Female Glossy Black-Cockatoo has reddish-yellow tail panel.

**HABITAT**
WOODLANDS
& FORESTS

**FOOD**
SEEDS
& BULBS

# Sulphur-crested Cockatoo

*Cacatua galerita* (= cockatoo with a crest)

**Length:** 45–50 cm

**Identification:** Medium to large white cockatoo with long, narrow, yellow crest, which is raised and fanned in excitement. Strong grey-black bill.

**Call:** Harsh screeching.

**Where found:** Forests and open country in northern and eastern Australia.

**Habits:** Gathers in large flocks when not breeding; feeds on seeds, bulbs, roots, insect larvae on ground in cooler part of day. When sitting around, may strip bark and leaves from trees.

**Nesting:** Nests in tree hollow, usually near water, sometimes in cliff holes. 2–3 white eggs incubated 30 days.

**Notes:** These cockatoos are sociable and endlessly active; it is sad to see one in a small cage. To nest, they need large old trees with big hollows.

**Status:** Common.

**Similar species:** Corellas have pale bills, lack yellow crest.

**HABITAT**
WOODLANDS
& FORESTS

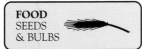
**FOOD**
SEEDS
& BULBS

# Rainbow Lorikeet

*Trichoglossus haematodus* (= hair-tongued blood-red bird)

**Length:** 30–32 cm

**Identification:** Medium-sized lorikeet with red bill, blue head, brilliant green upperparts, red-gold breastband and blue belly.

**Call:** Metallic screech.

**Where found:** Coastal lowlands of northern and eastern Australia, especially on flowering trees. Perth, WA.

**Habits:** Swift-flying, noisy flocks search for flowering trees. Birds feed with tongues tipped with "hairs", which mop up nectar. Also eat fruit, seeds, insects. Roost in camps, chattering and screeching before settling to sleep.

**Nesting:** Pairs for life. Nest in tree hollow; female incubates 2 white eggs 28 days, fed by male. Both parents feed young.

**Notes:** Introduced to Perth, WA, and now breeds there. Comes to garden feeders, even in large towns.

**Status:** Common.

**Similar species:** Scaly-breasted Lorikeet flocks with Rainbow, but has "scaly" green and gold breast.

**HABITAT**
FORESTS &
SUBURBS

**FOOD**
NECTAR
& SEEDS

# Crimson Rosella

*Platycercus elegans* (= flat-tailed, elegant bird)

**Length:** 32–36 cm

**Identification:** Medium-sized parrot with red head, rump, and underparts; back is mottled red and black. Cheek patches, outer wing feathers and tail are blue. In eastern SA, some birds have yellow replacing red.

**Call:** Screeching; bell-like chiming; chattering.

**Where found:** Edges of forest and woodland in eastern and southeastern coastal Australia, from Cairns, Qld, to SA.

**Habits:** Flocks wander forest edges looking for seeds and fruit, feeding in trees and on ground. Young ones roam more widely than mated adult pairs.

**Nesting:** Pair for life. Courting bird spreads and wags tail (see Pale-headed Rosella p. 8). Female incubates 4–5 white eggs in tree hollow for 19–21 days; both parents feed chicks.

**Notes:** May become very tame around camp grounds and picnic spots.

**Status:** Common.

**Similar species:** King-Parrot is larger and has green back.

**HABITAT**
WOODLANDS
& FORESTS

**FOOD**
FRUITS
& SEEDS

# Wonga Pigeon

*Leucosarca melanoleuca* (= white-meated, black and white bird)

**Length:** 38–40 cm

**Identification:** Medium-sized, plump, ground-living pigeon with grey upperparts, white face, white V mark on breast, white belly speckled black. Bill is red, tip brown; feet are pink.

**Call:** Loud *coo* repeated twice a second up to 100 times.

**Where found:** Dense coastal forests, from Rockhampton, Qld to Melbourne, Vic.

**Habits:** Alone or in pairs, feeding on seeds and fruit on forest floor. Flushes with loud clap of wings.

**Nesting:** Courting male stands on ground or log, swinging tail up and down, tucking head behind each spread wing in turn, showing off boldly marked breast. Nest a platform of twigs in tree, vine or fern. 2 white eggs are incubated 17–18 days.

**Notes:** Has disappeared as habitat destroyed. Once prized for eating, because its flesh remains white when cooked.

**Status:** Common in suitable habitat.

**Similar species:** Only forest-dwelling pigeon with broad white V on breast.

**HABITAT** COASTAL FORESTS

**FOOD** FRUITS & SEEDS

# Crested Pigeon

*Ocyphaps lophotes* (= swift pigeon with a crest)

**Length:** 30–34 cm

**Identification:** Medium-sized grey pigeon with crest on head, coloured speculum[G] on each black-barred wing, pink legs. Takes off with loud whistling of wings, then alternately flaps and glides.

**Call:** Cooing; sharp *wook*.

**Where found:** Dry grasslands near water on mainland Australia, avoiding dense forests. Common around farms.

**Habits:** Gathers in flocks to feed on ground on seed and at water.

**Nesting:** Nests after rainfall. Courting male bows and spreads wings and tail; in display flight, rises steeply up, then glides down again. Nest a frail stick platform in bush or tree; both parents incubate 2 white eggs for 18–20 days. Feed chicks "pigeon milk", then seed.

**Notes:** Has increased its range with human agriculture.

**Status:** Common.

**Similar species:** The 2 other crested pigeons have different habitats, Topknot in rainforest, Spinifex in central desert.

RAOUL SLATER

**HABITAT** GRASSLAND NEAR WATER

**FOOD** GRAINS & SEEDS

# Collared Sparrowhawk

*Accipiter cirrocephalus* (= tawny-headed hawk)

**Length:** ♀ 36–39 cm; ♂ 28–33cm

**Wingspan:** ♀ 80 cm; ♂ 55 cm

**Identification:** Small to medium-sized, long-tailed hawk with rounded wings and square-tipped tail. Grey upper-parts, rufous collar, barred rufous and white underparts. Round staring yellow eye.

**Call:** Repeated shrill *swee-swee-swee*.

**Where found:** Open woodland and forest, anywhere in Australia.

**Habits:** Dashes from cover at small birds, mammals, reptiles, seizing victim with long legs; carries prey to perch and plucks it before eating it.

**Nesting:** Stick nest in a tree fork. Male feeds female while she incubates 2–4 creamy, speckled eggs for 28–30 days. He then supplies food until the chicks are well grown and the female can hunt also.

**Notes:** Male is our smallest hawk. Fast, agile hunter.

Newly fledged[G] young bird has brown back, streaked brown-and-white breast.

**Status:** Common, but seldom seen.

**Similar species:** Australian Goshawk is larger, has rounded tailtip and "frowning" brow-ridges.

PETER SLATER

**HABITAT** WOODLANDS & FORESTS

**FOOD** SMALL BIRDS & MAMMALS

# Australian Kestrel

*Falco cenchroides* (= speckled falcon)

**Length:** ♀ 35 cm; ♂ 31 cm

**Wingspan:** ♀ 80 cm; ♂ 60 cm

**Identification:** Small to medium-sized falcon with long, pointed wings, rufous back, black bar near tailtip, yellow legs. Head of male blue-grey, of female brown streaked with black. Hovers[G] when hunting.

**Call:** Repeated shrill *ki-ki-ki*.

**Where found:** Open country, woodland, farms, towns and cities anywhere in Australia.

**Habits:** Perches or hovers, then pounces on mouse, insect or reptile. Turns up at insect and mouse plagues.

**Nesting:** Uses other birds' stick nests, tree hollows, cliffs or ledges of high buildings. 3–7 pale buff blotched eggs are incubated for 28 days by the female, who is fed by the male.

**Notes:** Female is larger than male. Lives anywhere prey and nest places exist. Harmless to

PETER SLATER

poultry. A farmer's friend.

**Status:** Common.

**Similar species:** Brown Falcon is larger, with longer, blue legs, scruffier appearance.

**HABITAT** FARMLANDS & OPEN SPACES

**FOOD** MICE & INSECTS

# Emu

*Dromaius novaehollandiae* (= fast-footed Australian)

**Height:** 1.5–1.9 m

**Weight:** 35–50 kg

**Identification:** Huge, long-legged, flightless bird. Soft, shaggy grey-brown feathers.

Pale blue skin on neck and face.

**Call:** Booming; drumming.

**Where found:** All over mainland Australia, except for rainforest.

**Habits:** Lives in small mobs. Eats green plants, seeds and insects.

**Nesting:** Male incubates[G] 5–15 dark green eggs on ground for about 55 days. Cares for striped chicks for up to 6 months.

**Notes:** Female larger than male. Inquisitive – wave a handkerchief to bring an emu close. Must drink regularly, so found within range of water. Farmed for leather, meat and oil. Three island species made extinct by early European settlers.

**Status[G]:** Common.

**Similar species[G]:** None.

HABITAT
ALL OVER
AUSTRALIA

FOOD
SEEDS &
INSECTS

# Southern Cassowary

*Casuarius casuarius* (= horned head)

**Height:** 1.5–1.7 m

**Weight:** ♀ 58 kg; ♂ 34 kg

**Identification:** Huge, stocky, flightless bird with glossy black feathers. Horny helmet. Bright blue skin on neck and face, red wattles.

**Call:** Hissing; booming; rumbling.

**Where found:** Rainforest in northeastern Qld.

**Habits:** Lives alone. Feeds on fallen fruits.

**Nesting:** Male incubates 3–4 pea-green eggs on ground for about 55 days. He then cares for the striped chicks.

**Notes:** Helmet protects head when dashing through forest. Inner toe has long sharp nail and kick can be dangerous.

**Status:** Threatened as its rainforest habitat disappears. Killed by dogs and vehicles.

**Similar species:** None.

STANLEY BREEDEN

**HABITAT**
NE QLD
RAINFOREST

**FOOD**
FALLEN
FRUITS

# Malleefowl

*Leipoa ocellata* (= eye-marked egg-leaver)

**Length:** 55 – 60 cm

**Weight:** 1.5 – 2.5 kg

**Identification:** Large, ground-dweller with strong legs. Mainly grey/fawn with brown bars and eye-like spots. Black stripes down pale breast.

**Call:** Male loud booming and grunts; female high-pitched crow.

**Where found:** In dry scrubby woodland and mallee shrubland in southern Aust.

**Habits:** Eats seeds, leaf buds and insects; may feed in small groups. Roosts in low bushes. Shy and wary, relies on camouflage.

**Nesting:** Pairs mate for life. Male builds huge mound of leaves and sand and regulates nest temperature during incubation. Female lays 10 to 35 eggs singly in 1 season. Eggs hatch in 7 weeks. Chicks are independent at birth.

**Notes:** Male spends most of time building and maintaining nest; female spends her time feeding in order to produce so many eggs.

**Status:** Vulnerable to habitat clearance and predators.

**Similar species:** None.

**HABITAT**
WOODLAND
& SHRUBLAND

**FOOD**
SEEDS &
INSECTS

# Australian Brush-turkey

*Alectura lathami* ( = Latham's cock-tailed bird)

**Length:** 60–75 cm

**Wingspan:** 85 cm

**Identification:** Large, black, strong-legged, ground-living bird with upright, fanlike tail. Grey edges to breast feathers. Naked red head; male wattle larger and bright yellow, female wattle smaller and paler.

**Call:** Grunting; male booms at nest mound.

**Where found:** Coastal rainforest, from Cape York south to Gosford, NSW.

**Habits:** Spends most of the day on the ground. Eats fruit, seed, insects.

**Nesting:** Male builds nest mound of plant litter and soil. Females visit a mound to lay eggs, then are driven away. Male adds or removes material to keep mound at 33°C . Eggs take about 50 days to hatch, then chicks look after themselves.

**Notes:** Shy in the forest, but where habitat destruction pushes it into suburbs may become very tame. Mound can take over a garden, but daily care of nest is fascinating to watch. Roosts in trees.

**Status:** Common, but threatened by habitat destruction.

**Similar species:** None.

**HABITAT**
RAINFOREST
& ITS EDGES

**FOOD**
FRUITS
& SEEDS

# Australian Bustard

*Ardeotis australis* (= southern heron-bustard)

**Length:** ♀ 80 cm; ♂ 1.1–1.2 m

**Wingspan:** ♀ 1.7 m; ♂ 2.3 m

**Identification:** Very large, long-legged, plains bird with brown back, white neck and breast. Male has black crown, female has brown crown.

**Call:** Booming; roaring.

**Where found:** Grassland, especially in drier northern Australia.

**Habits:** Feeds during day on plains on grass, seeds, insects such as grasshoppers, and small animals such as mice. When aware of danger it freezes, then walks slowly away.

**Nesting:** Male displays with throat pouch blown up, wings drooping, head and tail thrown up, strutting and booming. Female incubates 1–2 spotted eggs on ground alone, creeping away if disturbed, then cares for chicks by herself.

**Notes:** Member of a group becoming rare worldwide. Hunting by humans and foxes, and habitat destruction by sheep and rabbits have reduced numbers greatly. Good flier and may arrive after rainfall.

**Status:** Disappearing. Needs protection.

**Similar species:** Bush Stone-curlew is much smaller; it rests during the day and is active at night.

**HABITAT** GRASS-LAND

**FOOD** SEEDS & ANIMALS

# Masked Lapwing

*Vanellus miles* (= fan-winged soldier)

**Length:** 33–38 cm

**Wingspan:** 75–85 cm

**Identification:** Medium-sized, long-legged wader with grey-brown back, black from forehead down back and sides of neck, white throat and belly. Yellow forehead, mask and wattles. Spur on bend of wing.

**Call:** Piercing alarm call *keer-kek-kee-kee*.

**Where found:** Grasslands near water, in northern, eastern and central Australia.

**Habits:** In pairs or small groups, hunting for insects, other animals and seeds in short grass.

**Nesting:** Both parents incubate 3–4 blotched eggs in scrape on ground for 28 days. Chicks leave nest soon after hatching.

**Notes:** Clearing land has provided more habitat and Masked Lapwing may breed in towns. Defends eggs and chicks by diving vigorously.

**Status:** Common.

**Similar species:** Banded Lapwing has shorter legs, black "bib", red wattle between eye and bill.

PETER SLATER

**HABITAT** GRASSLANDS & WETLANDS

**FOOD** INSECTS & SEEDS

# Black Swan

*Cygnus atratus* (= black swan)

**Length:** 1.1–1.4 m

**Wingspan:** 1.6–2.0 m

**Identification:** Very large black swan; white wing-tips, red bill.

**Call:** Bugling; soft crooning.

**Where found:** On or near water, anywhere in Australia.

**Habits:** Usually in flocks. Feeds on water weed and other plants near water.

**Nesting:** Pair builds nest of reeds and grasses on ground or in shallow water. 4–10 greenish eggs are incubated for up to 45 days. Cygnets stay with parents for 5–6 months.

**Notes:** Nests after rain. Can fly long distances. Flightless flocks gather on water while moulting⁶. Feed and sometimes breed on city lakes.

**Status:** Common on wetlands.

**Similar species:** Mute Swan (introduced species) white, with black face.

 **HABITAT** NEAR OR ON WATER

 **FOOD** WATER PLANTS

# Australasian Grebe

*Tachybaptus novaehollandiae* (= Australian fast-diver)

RAOUL SLATER

**Length:** 23–25 cm

**Wingspan:** 39 cm

**Identification:** Small, grey-brown waterbird with short bill, short neck, plump body. Yellow patch on head when breeding. Lobed toes. Dives when disturbed.

**Call:** Trills when courting.

**Where found:** Freshwater wetlands, farm dams, town lakes.

**Habits:** Dives for fish, snails, other water animals.

**Nesting:** Small, round, floating platform of waterweed. Usually 4 eggs, incubated by both parents for 23 days and covered with weed when they leave nest. Chicks stay with parents 8 weeks.

**Notes:** In pairs or small groups. Stays under water up to 20 seconds. Adults carry chicks on their backs. Grebes eat feathers to stop fishbones damaging stomachs.

**Status:** Common in suitable habitat.

**Similar species:** Hoary-headed Grebe paler, with white streaks on head.

**HABITAT**
WETLANDS
& LAKES

**FOOD**
FISH &
WATER LIFE

# Australian Pelican

*Pelecanus conspicillatus* (= spectacled pelican)

**Length:** 1.6–1.8 m

**Wingspan:** 2.3–2.5 m

**Weight:** 4–6.8 kg

**Identification:** Very large, short-legged, white and black bird with huge pink bill. All four toes webbed.

**Call:** Soft grunt; groan.

**Where found:** Anywhere there are water and fish.

**Habits:** Feeds on fish scooped up in bill and throat pouch. May hunt in large group.

**Nesting:** Nests on islands. Two eggs laid on ground, brooded by parents in turn for 32–35 days. At 25 days chicks join group "nurseries". They can fly at 3 months.

**Notes:** Flies high and far in search of fishing grounds. May breed in great numbers on inland lakes after rain.

**Status:** Common where fish are available.

**Similar species:** None.

**HABITAT**
FRESH &
SALT WATER

**FOOD**
FISH

# Australian Darter

*Anhinga melanogaster* (= black-bellied darter)

**Length:** 86–94 cm

**Wingspan:** 1.2 m

**Weight:** 1–2.6 kg

**Identification:** Large waterbird with thin, kinked neck. Sits upright, often with wings outstretched. Male glossy black; female grey-brown above, whitish below; young very pale.

**Call:** Rattling clicking; hiss.

**Where found:** Usually on still, deep fresh water. Sometimes on salt water.

**Habits:** Spears fish underwater, surfaces to shake them off bill and swallow. Perches with outstretched wings.

**Nesting:** Large stick nest in tree over water. Male and female both build, then incubate 4 pale green eggs for 28 days. Both feed young, who fledge in about 50 days.

**Notes:** Swims with only its "snaky" neck and slender head above surface. Sinks without

splash when alarmed.

**Status:** Common on suitable habitat.

**Similar species:** 4 species of cormorant, which have shorter, thicker necks and stouter, hooked bills.

**HABITAT**
DEEP FRESH
WATER

**FOOD**
FRESH-
WATER FISH

# Australian White Ibis

*Threskiornis molucca* (= sacred Moluccan bird)

PETER SLATER

to side in water while wading, seizing water animals; also takes grasshoppers, small snakes, worms. Probes manure.

**Nesting:** Builds in flooded swamps. Courting male shows off scarlet patches under wings. Nest a stick platform in reed clump or bush; parent birds incubate 2–5 white eggs in turn for 20–25 days.

**Notes:** Flock flies in V-formation, all birds flapping then gliding together. When feeding, may hammer mussel shells open with bill. Very adaptable bird, which may scavenge for food in parks, zoos etc.

**Status:** Common.

**Similar species:** Straw-necked Ibis has glossy black back. Royal and Yellow-billed Spoonbills have broad, spoon-ended bills.

**Length:** 69–76 cm

**Identification:** Large, white (sometimes dirty), wading bird with naked, black neck and head, long, downcurved bill.

**Call:** Grunting *urk*.

**Where found:** Wetlands.

**Habits:** Moves head from side

**HABITAT**
WETLANDS
& SWAMPS

**FOOD**
SMALL
ANIMALS

# Cattle Egret

*Ardea ibis* (= heron-ibis)

**Length:** 48-53 cm

**Identification:** Medium-sized, stocky, short-necked, white heron. Bill and feet pale yellow. When breeding, has orange-buff neck and back and red bill.

**Call:** Croaks at nest.

**Where found:** Wetlands and grazing lands around coastal Australia.

**Habits:** Usually with cattle or horses, feeding on insects, frogs and other small animals. Roosts in groups over water.

**Nesting:** Nests in large colonies with other waterbirds. Male chooses site in tree, attracts female by raising plumes[G], waving nesting sticks. 3-6 pale blue eggs are incubated for 22 - 26 days by both parents.

**Notes:** Commonly seen with large grazing animals, sometimes on their backs. Probably introduced itself into northern Australia about 1940 and has spread to all States. (It does not breed in Vic. or Tas.)

**Status:** Common, increasing.

**Similar species:** Little Egret more slender, with black bill and yellow face.

RAOUL SLATER

**HABITAT**
WETLANDS
PASTURES

**FOOD**
SMALL
ANIMALS

# Black-necked Stork (Jabiru)

*Ephippiorhynchus asiaticus* (= Asian horse-billed bird)

**Height:** 1.2 m

**Wingspan:** 2 m

**Identification:** Very large, black and white, black-necked wading bird with red legs, strong black bill. Male eye dark, female eye yellow.

**Call:** Clatters bill.

**Where found:** Wetlands across northern Australia, south to Sydney, NSW.

**Habits:** Alone or in a pair, stalking fish, snakes, frogs etc. in shallow water or wet grass. Soars high in air.

**Nesting:** Nest a huge stick platform in tall tree in swamp. 2–3 white eggs are incubated by both parents.

**Notes:** Australia's only stork. Pairs for life. Large area of wetland needed to support one pair. Habitat threatened by coastal development.

**Status:** Disappearing.

**Similar species:** None.

**HABITAT** WETLANDS & SWAMPS

**FOOD** WETLANDS ANIMALS

# Brolga

*Grus rubicunda* (= reddish crane)

**Length:** ♀ 95–115 cm;
♂ 105–125 cm

**Wingspan:** 1.7–2.4 m

**Identification:** Very large, long-legged, pale grey crane with bare red skin on head and grey-green crown. Grey legs.

**Call:** Trumpeting.

**Where found:** Wetlands and wet grasslands across northern, western and eastern Australia.

**Habits:** Small group or large flocks feed on swampland tubers[G] dug up with bills; may eat grain and insects. Wanders widely, may fly at great height.

**Nesting:** Nest a platform of grass and reeds about 1.5 m across. Both parents incubate 2 white eggs for 28–30 days. Young remain with their parents for up to 1 year.

**Notes:** Flocks are made up of family groups, each led by a male. Famous for dramatic and graceful "dancing".

**Status:** Common in north, but disappearing from southeastern Australia.

**Similar species:** Sarus Crane has pink legs; red skin extends down its upper neck.

**HABITAT**
WETLANDS
& PLAINS

**FOOD**
TUBERS &
INSECTS

# Purple Swamphen

*Porphyrio porphyrio* (= purple purple-bird)

**Length:** 44–48 cm

**Wingspan:** 70–88 cm

**Identification:** Large, black-backed, blue or purple-breasted wading bird. Has stout red legs, big feet, and a strong scarlet bill and forehead shield. Flicks tail to show white beneath.

**Call:** Loud screeching, usually made at night.

**Where found:** Freshwater wetlands, near reedbeds and nearby pasture, in northern, eastern and southwestern Australia.

**Habits:** Climbs through reeds, can swim, and runs fast. Rests on roosting platforms. Main diet young reed stems, bitten off then held in foot. Also eats other plants, eggs and small water animals.

**Nesting:** Group of birds makes a reed platform nest, in which several females may lay. All incubate 3–8 blotched eggs for 23–29 days.

**Notes:** Lives in pairs or flocks. Sometimes perches in trees. May prey on young water-birds, frogs etc. Becomes tame on parklands.

**Status:** Common.

**Similar species:** Dusky Moorhen is black, with slender, yellow-tipped red bill.

 **HABITAT**
WETLANDS & SWAMPS

 **FOOD**
PLANTS, ANIMALS

# Comb-crested Jacana

*Irediparra gallinula* (= Iredale's fowl-like bird)

**Length:** 20–24 cm
(female larger than male)

**Identification:** Small to medium waterbird with long slender legs and enormously long toes. Brown back and wings, white neck and belly. Comb on forehead red, orange or yellow.

**Call:** Trumpeting alarm; piping.

**Where found:** Permanent freshwater ponds and lagoons in northern and eastern Australia, south to Grafton, NSW.

**Habits:** Runs over floating plants, head bobbing, tail flicking. Eats seeds and shoots and small water animals.

**Nesting:** Nest is a frail raft of plant stems anchored to water plants. Female courts male, who incubates 3–4 squiggled eggs and looks after chicks.

**Notes:** Also known as "lily-trotter". Jacanas may escape danger under water. Adult may shift eggs or downy young by carrying them under their wings, legs dangling.

**Status:** Common in suitable habitat.

**Similar species:** None.

**HABITAT**
PONDS &
LAGOONS

**FOOD**
SEEDS &
WATER-LIFE

# Crested Tern

*Sterna bergii* (= Bergius's tern)

**Length:** 46–49 cm

**Identification:** Medium-sized, white seabird with grey back and wings; short legs; black crown; crested nape; yellow bill. Graceful flier, with slender pointed wings and a forked tail. Dives from some height.

**Call:** Rasping "krreck".

**Range:** Australian coasts.

**Habits:** Dives for fish from 5–15 m above water; rests on sand at high tide with other terns and gulls.

**Nesting:** Nests in colonies; 1–2 mottled eggs laid in scrape on sand; both parents incubate 25–26 days and care for chicks.

**Notes:** Commonest Australian tern. Diving terns indicate schools of small surface fish.

**Status:** Common.

**Similar species:** Lesser Crested Tern much smaller.

**HABITAT**
SEA &
COASTS

**FOOD**
MARINE
FISH

# Silver Gull

*Larus novaehollandiae* (= Australian gull)

**Length:** 38–43 cm

**Wingspan:** 90 cm

**Identification:** White seabird; adult has grey wings, red legs and beak. Young has brown on back and wings.

**Where found:** Around southern coasts and on inland waters.

**Habits:** Gathers in flocks where food is available, near harbours, public beaches, parks. Bold and aggressive.

**Nesting:** Breeds on offshore islands in dense colonies. Nest is on ground; 2–3 eggs hatch in 21–27 days. Both parents incubate and feed chicks.

**Notes:** Feeds on fish, scavenges[G] garbage, takes other birds' eggs and chicks. Roosts[G] in large flocks.

**Status:** Common on southern coasts, some inland waters.

**Similar species:** Same-size terns have slender wings, black caps, forked tails.

**HABITAT**
SEA
COASTS

**FOOD**
FISH; IS A
SCAVENGER

# Pied Oystercatcher

*Haemantopus longirostris* (= red-footed long-billed bird)

**Length:** 48–52 cm

**Wingspan:** 85–95 cm

**Identification:** Medium-sized, black and white wading bird with long, scarlet bill and eye-ring, and dull red legs.

**Call:** Sharp, carrying alarm call *pit-a-peep*.

**Where found:** Sandy ocean beaches around Australia.

**Habits:** Alone or in pairs on tideline, pushing bill into sand, feeding on shellfish, worms and crabs. Roosts and rests in flocks.

**Nesting:** Pair mates for life. Both incubate 2–3 spotted eggs in scrape on sand for 28–32 days. Pretend injury to lead danger from nest or chicks.

**Notes:** Opens bivalve molluscs by stabbing to cut muscles holding shell or hammering shells until one breaks. Chicks are taught by parents to prise or hammer.

**Status:** Common.

**Similar species:** The similarly shaped Sooty Oystercatcher is all-black and usually lives on rocky shores.

**HABITAT**
OCEAN
BEACHES

**FOOD**
MOLLUSCS
& SHORE-LIFE

# Little Penguin

*Eudyptula minor* (= small good-diver)

**Length:** 40–45 cm

**Weight:** about 1 kg

**Identification:** Medium-sized (but smallest penguin). Blue-grey above, white below.

**Call:** Yaps; grunts; brays.

**Where found:** In sea off southern coast, or nesting on beach.

**Habits:** Feeds at sea on fish and other marine animals.

**Nesting:** Nests on islands or coastal beach, in burrow in sand or under rocks. Two white eggs are brooded by parents in turn for 36 days. Chicks go to sea about 56 days after hatching.

**Notes:** Only penguin to breed in Australia. Parents come to shore to feed chicks at dusk, go to sea at dawn. Adults moult in burrows. Threatened by oil

spills, habitat disturbance.

**Status:** Not common. Breeding areas need protection.

**Similar species:** Rockhopper and Fiordland Penguins are larger and have yellow crests.

**HABITAT**
SEA &
COAST

**FOOD**
MARINE
FISH

109

# Reptiles

An animal is a reptile if it:

- has a backbone and a skull
- is cold-blooded and has a four-chambered heart
- has lungs and breathes air
- has scales that grow from its dry skin
- produces eggs laid on land or hatched in the female's body

## Reptile Groups

Australian reptiles can be divided into three main groups:
Crocodilia, Testudines and Squamata.

### Crocodilia – crocodiles

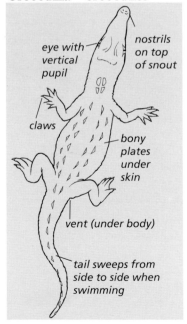

eye with vertical pupil

nostrils on top of snout

claws

bony plates under skin

vent (under body)

tail sweeps from side to side when swimming

### Testudines – turtles

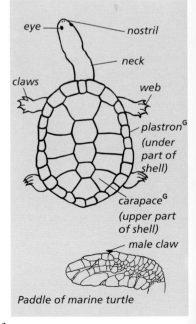

eye

nostril

neck

claws

web

plastron[G] (under part of shell)

carapace[G] (upper part of shell)

male claw

Paddle of marine turtle

110

# Squamata – lizards and snakes

| ALL SNAKES | MOST LIZARDS | A FEW LIZARDS |
|---|---|---|
| lack limbs (pythons have traces) | have limbs | have reduced or no limbs, or hindlimb flaps |
| lack ear-openings | have ear-openings or tympanums | have scaly depressions instead of ear openings |
| have long, slender, forked tongues | have fleshy tongues which may be notched | have long, slender forked tongues (monitors) |
| lack eyelids | have movable lower eyelids | have immovable lower eyelids (legless lizards, geckos and some skinks) |
| lack ability to shed tail | lack ability to shed tail (monitors, dragons, some large skinks) | can shed tail and regrow part or all of it |
| have tails that are shorter than head plus body | have tails that are longer than head plus body | have tails that are shorter than head plus body |
| have single or enlarged belly scales (except file snakes and blind snakes) | have small underbody scales that are nearly equal in size to body scales | have large underbody scales arranged in pairs (some legless lizards) |

# Australian Freshwater Crocodile

*Crocodylus johnstoni* (= Johnstone's crocodile)

**Length:** HBT up to 3 m

**Identification:** Comparatively slender crocodile. Upper surface grey to green-brown with darker markings. Underside is whitish. Snout is long, slender and smooth; teeth are slender and sharp.

**Where found:** Permanent fresh water (billabongs, swamps, rivers) in northern and northeastern Aust. Occasionally in tidal waters, or walking overland at night between bodies of water.

**Habits:** Found where plants or rocks overhang water. Basks on banks or in shallow water, but spends most of its time in the water. From sunset, hunts small animals, including insects, fish, frogs, birds and reptiles, in the water. Female lays 12–20 eggs in a nest in a sandbank towards end of Dry season (Oct.–Nov.). A female (may not be mother) digs out the nest when young hatch, and may carry them to water in her mouth.

**Notes:** Not harmful to humans. However, will bite if seized or interfered with.

**Status:** Secure.

**Similar species:** Small Saltwater Crocodile has broad, bumpy snout.

**HABITAT** SWAMPS & RIVERS

**FOOD** MAINLY WATER LIFE

# Saltwater (Estuarine) Crocodile

*Crocodylus porosus* (= pore-skinned crocodile)

**Length:** HBT up to 7 m

**Identification:** Small to enormous crocodile. Upper surface brown, grey or nearly black with dark markings. Underside whitish. Snout short in comparison to width, broad and has grainy, bumpy surface.

**Where found:** Sea, estuaries, swamps, rivers and floodplains in northern Aust.

**Habits:** Basks or shelters in shade along banks during day, hunts animals in or near water at night. Large male holds a territory[G]. Female mates early in Wet season, lays up to 60 hard-shelled eggs in nest of vegetation on river bank. She later cares for the hatchlings.

**Notes:** A potential danger to humans. Numbers recovering since hunting stopped in 1970s.

**Status:** Secure.

**Similar species:** Freshwater Crocodile has slender snout.

**HABITAT**
FRESH &
SALT WATER

**FOOD**
LAND OR
WATER LIFE

# Krefft's River Turtle

*Emydura krefftii* (= Krefft's fresh-water tortoise)

**Length:** Carapace to 25 cm

**Identification:** Freshwater turtle with broad, oval shell. Brown to dark brown above; cream below. Cream stripe along lower jaw and behind eye. Head and neck shorter than carapace. Front feet webbed with 5 clawed digits.

**Where found:** Large rivers and permanent waterholes in eastern Qld. In lakes on Fraser Island.

**Habits:** Feeds on plants, crustaceans, insects and molluscs. Clutch of 4–16 eggs laid in sandy banks.

**Notes:** Juvenile has serrated, white-edged shell. Were and are an Aboriginal food source. Fraser Island turtles are smaller and have adapted to acidic water in perched lakes.

**Status:** Common.

**Similar species:** *E. subglobosa* has red stripe on lower jaw, red leg spots and shell margins.

**HABITAT**
RIVERS & WATERHOLES

**FOOD**
PLANTS & INSECTS

# Eastern Snake-necked Turtle

*Chelodina longicollis* (= long-necked little tortoise)

**Length:** Carapace to 25 cm

**Identification:** Dinner-plate-sized, long-necked freshwater turtle with head plus neck measurement as long as, or longer than, shell length. Carapace brown or black, with black seams between its plates. Head flattened, eyes look sideways, nostrils on tip of snout. Front foot webbed, with 4 clawed digits.

**Where found:** Coastal and inland wetlands and rivers, from eastern Qld to southeastern SA.

**Habits:** Basks on sandbank or submerged log. Feeds on animals found in water. In summer, may wander in search of water, or burrow into mud and aestivate.

Female lays 12 or more brittle-shelled eggs in hole in earth bank in early summer. Hatchlings emerge up to 5 months later, after rain has dampened nest.

**Notes:** When underwater, pushes nostrils above surface in order to breathe.

**Status:** Secure.

**Similar species:** Very large Broad-shelled Snake-necked Turtle, *C. expansa*, found in Murray-Darling River system and coastal central Qld.

**HABITAT**
RIVERS &
WETLANDS

**FOOD**
WATER &
OTHER LIFE

# Western Swamp Turtle

*Pseudemydura umbrina* (= shaded false *Emydura*\*)

JIRI LOCHMAN

**Length:** Carapace to 15 cm

**Identification:** Saucer-sized, short-necked, freshwater turtle. Brown carapace is almost square in outline. Plastron pale with dark seams between plates. Head and neck much shorter than shell; head broad and flat and protected by horny shield. Front feet webbed with 5 clawed digits.

**Where found:** One small swamp at Ellenbrook, north of Perth, WA.

**Habits:** Lives in an area of summer drought and winter rain. Spends 6–9 months of each year aestivating under soil or in ground litter. Becomes active when its habitat is flooded with water, which needs to be above 14°C in temperature.

**Notes:** A hatchling needs to grow for 2 seasons before aestivating successfully. It may not breed until over 15 years of age. This is Australia's rarest reptile, which needs protection. A captive breeding program is under way.

**Status:** Rare and endangered.

**Similar species:** None.

\* Emydura is another genus of short-necked turtles.

HABITAT
PAPERBARK
SWAMP

FOOD
WATER
LIFE

# Pitted-shelled Turtle

*Carettochelys insculpta* (=engraved tortoise-shell tortoise)

**Length:** Carapace to 70 cm

**Identification:** Shell covered with soft, pitted skin. Grey to grey-brown above, cream below. Pale streak behind eye. Webbed, paddle-like feet with 2 claws. Nostrils at end of prominent snout.

**Where found:** Freshwater rivers, lagoons and billabongs in northern NT.

**Habits:** Feeds on snails, small fish and fruit. Totally aquatic; female only leaves water to nest. Clutch of 8–30 eggs laid in sandbanks. Young turtles remain dormant in eggs until nest floods during wet season.

**Note:** Well-known to Aborigines, but only discovered by scientists in 1969. Also called Pig-nosed Turtle.

**Status:** Common, but distribution limited.

**Similar species:** None.

**HABITAT**
RIVERS &
LAGOONS

**FOOD**
WATER LIFE
& FRUIT

# Green Turtle

*Chelonia mydas* (= *mydas\* tortoise*)

**Length:** Carapace up to 1 m

**Identification:** Large sea turtle with an olive-green, high-domed carapace mottled with darker brown and black, and a pale plastron. Shell may be oval or almost heart-shaped. Head of an adult is small in relation to its body size.

**Where found:** Coral reefs and seagrass flats, in tropical and warm temperate waters along northern coasts of Aust.

**Habits:** Feeds on seaweeds and seagrasses. May return 1000 km to nest site. Female mates in water and may explore a beach before digging a hole above high tide mark and laying up to 200 soft-shelled eggs in it. More clutches laid at intervals of up to 15 days. Eggs hatch in 54–70 days.

**Notes:** This is the only vegetarian turtle and it is a traditional human food. Outside Aust., flesh and eggs eaten, shell used for jewellery, skin for leather, oil for cosmetics. In danger from fishing nets, powerboats.

**Status:** Decreasing in numbers.

**Similar species:** None.

\* Meaning of mydas unknown.

**HABITAT**
OCEANS &
COASTS

**FOOD**
SEAWEED,
SEAGRASS

# Loggerhead Turtle

*Caretta caretta* (= tortoise-shell turtle)

**Length:** Carapace to 1.5 m

**Identification:** Large to enormous sea turtle, with dark reddish-brown carapace, speckled darker, and pale plastron. Adult head is massive, jaws powerful and flippers small (compared with heads and flippers of other sea turtle species).

**Where found:** Tropical and warm temperate waters around northern Aust.

**Habits:** Feeds on molluscs, crabs, sea urchins (helped by large jaw muscles) and sea jellies. Female mates in sea, then lays up to 125 eggs in a pit dug above high tide mark. After 60–80 days, hatchlings dig from nest at night and make their way to the sea.

**Notes:** One of the 4 species of sea turtle which nests regularly along Qld coast. Main South Pacific nest site is on Wreck Island, in the Capricorn Bunker Group, Qld; mainland nest site is at Mon Repos, near Bundaberg, Qld. Hatchlings are reddish-brown above, dark blackish-brown below.

**Status:** Rare and endangered.

**Similar species:** No other sea turtle has such a massive head.

**HABITAT**
OCEAN & COAST

**FOOD**
MOLLUSCS & SEA LIFE

# Flatback Turtle

*Natator depressus* (= pressed-down swimmer)

**Length:** Carapace to 1.2 m.

**Identification:** Large sea turtle with flattened shell covered by skin. Broad, heart-shaped carapace with upturned edges; grey to olive. Cream below extending to neck and sides of head. Hatchlings are olive with black-edged scutes.

**Where found:** Beaches, coastal waters and offshore cays in northern Australia.

**Habits:** Feeds on marine invertebrates. Female lays clutches of up to 60 eggs at a time from Oct. to Jan. Eggs take 8 weeks to hatch.

**Notes:** Cape York is an important nesting ground.

**Status:** Limited distribution; occurs only in Australia.

**Similar species:** Green and Loggerhead hatchlings are half the size of Flatback hatchlings.

 **HABITAT** OCEANS & COASTS

 **FOOD** MARINE INVERTEBRATES

# Leathery Turtle

*Dermochelys coriacea* (= leathery-skinned turtle)

**Length:** Carapace to 3 m.

**Identification:** Very large sea turtle. Heavy limbs without webbing or claws. Pointed shell is a mosaic of small, flat bones embedded in leathery skin. Dark brown to black above with paler blotches and 7 lengthwise ridges. Throat and lower neck pale with dark blotches. Hatchlings blue-black with white beading and edges.

**Where found:** All coastal waters. Most commonly seen in large bays, estuaries and rivers in temperate areas.

**Habits:** Feeds on sea jellies. Nests occasionally on central Qld coast and in Arnhem Land, NT. Clutches of 60–100 round eggs laid.

**Status:** Protected species in Australia.

**Notes:** Can dive to depths of 1000 m. Burns fat to maintain higher body temperature than surroundings. World's largest sea turtle.

**Similar species:** None.

**HABITAT**
COASTAL
WATERS

**FOOD**
SEA JELLIES

# Lizards

## What sort of lizard is it?

A key to the families of Australian lizards:

**1** Eyes either with movable lids or without movable lids

Has limbs (which may be small) .................................**go to 2**

Has no limbs; there may be a scaly flap instead ..........**go to 5**

**2** Eyes with or without movable lids:
- Pupil is not a vertical slit in daylight
- Scales on head and neck are overlapping..............**go to 3**

Eyes without movable lids:
- Pupil is a vertical slit in daylight
- Scales on head and neck lie side by side ...............**geckos**

*(over 100 Australian species)*

**3** Scales on the top of the head are tiny and irregular ..........**go to 4**

Scales on the top of the head are large, regular
and shield-like ...............................................................**skinks**

*(over 300 Australian species)*

**4** Tongue is long, slender, deeply forked, often flickered
in and out when owner is alert ..............................**monitors**

*(over 25 Australian species)*

Tongue is broad and flat with a small notch in front:
Appears when owner eats and drinks .....................**dragons**

*(over 60 Australian species)*

**5** Eyes are without movable eyelids ..........................**legless lizards**

*(over 30 Australian species)*

Eyes have eyelids.....................................................**some skinks**

# Northern Leaf-tailed Gecko

*Phyllurus cornutus* (= horned leaf-tail)

**Length:** HB to 16 cm

**Identification:** Large gecko with flattened leaf-shaped tail. Large triangular head with V-shaped markings. Olive-green to brown above with 4–5 pale blotches with dark edges across back; dark brown flecks and mottling. Often has reddish stripe down back. Spines along flanks. Long limbs with slender, clawed digits.

**Where found:** Cairns to Townsville region of NE Qld. in rainforest and wet eucalypt forests on coast and ranges.

**Habits:** Shelters in hollows and under bark. Forages on trees for insects and spiders at night. Two eggs laid in tree hollows.

**Notes:** Can change colour to match surroundings. Can regrow damaged tail.

**Status:** Common.

**Similar species:** Southern Leaf-tailed Gecko has different range.

IAN MORRIS

**HABITAT**
HOLLOWS & BARK

**FOOD**
INSECTS & SPIDERS

123

# Variegated Dtella

*Gehyra variegata* (= variegated *Gehyra*\*)

**Length:** HB to 5.5 cm; T to 7cm

**Identification:** Medium-sized, soft-skinned gecko with flattened body and depression at base of tail. Upper surface grey or grey-brown with many darker markings. Underside whitish. Lidless eye has a vertical pupil. Digits expanded into large pads; all but the innermost bear claws.

**Where found:** From coastal WA (except southwestern corner and Kimberley) across interior of Aust.

**Habits:** Spends the day under loose bark or in a tree hollow, under a rock flake or in a crevice of a building. At night roams sloping and vertical surfaces, hunting insects and spiders. Female lays 1 egg, often in a nest with other females' eggs.

**Notes:** Changes colour from darker during day to paler at night. Able to lose tail and later regrow it. Cleans eyes with tongue. Several may share a daytime shelter.

**Status:** Secure.

**Similar species:** Dubious Dtella, G. *dubia*, in coastal Qld and northern NSW; Top-end Dtella, G. *australis*, in northern NT, WA.

\* Meaning of *Gehyra* is unknown.

IAN MORRIS

**HABITAT**
TREES, ROCKS
& HOUSES

**FOOD**
INSECTS,
SPIDERS

# Three-lined Knob-tailed Gecko

*Nephrurus levis* (= smooth kidney-tail)

JIRI LOCHMAN

**Length:** HB to 9 cm; T to 5.4 cm

**Identification:** Large, big-headed gecko with a short, fat tail ending in a small knob. Upper surface purple-brown with white tubercles in lines. Yellowish bars across head, neck and shoulder. Underside white. Digits end in claws.

**Where found:** In dry, sandy country, open woodland and grassland from central coast of WA to arid interiors of all mainland States except Vic.

**Habits:** Shelters during day and in cold weather in a tunnel it has dug in the side of another animal's burrow, or in its own burrow. At night, hunts insects, spiders, scorpions and other geckos. Remains able to run fast when cold slows other lizards.

**Notes:** Knobbed tail vibrated and twitched in alarm or aggression. Tail not easily shed.

**Status:** Secure.

**Similar species:** Smooth Knob-tail Gecko, *N. laevissimus*, has dark bars across head, neck and upper back.

**HABITAT**
DRY
INLAND

**FOOD**
SMALL LIFE,
GECKOS

# Spiny-tailed Gecko

*Diplodactylus ciliaris* (= eyelashed double-toe)

**Length:** HBT to 15 cm

**Identification:** Varies from silvery-grey with scattered orange and black spots to reddish-brown mottled with grey, orange and white. Usually two rows of orange and brown spines along back and tail. Fringe of spines on eyebrow and iris of eye is patterned.

**Where found:** From coastal monsoon forests in north-west Aust. to woodlands and spinifex grassland in central Aust.

**Habits:** Feeds at night on insects. Shelters during day under tree bark or spinifex clumps. Two eggs per clutch.

**Notes:** Deters predators by squirting sticky fluid from base of spines and tail up to 30 cm.

**Status:** Common.

**Similar species:** None.

IAN MORRIS

 **HABITAT** FORESTS & WOODLANDS

**FOOD** INSECTS

*Oedura marmorata* (= marbled swollen-tail)

**Length:** HBT to 18 cm

**Identification:** Brown to purplish-brown with 5 or 6 broken bands of yellow or white across back. Sides speckled white, yellow and brown. Pale stripe along lips. Some adults have no banding. Juveniles are dark with distinct yellow or cream bands and little or no speckling. Digits are long with distinct pads.

**Where found:** Central and northern Australia in grassy woodlands, spinifex grassland and rocky outcrops.

**Habits:** Feeds on insects and small lizards. Shelters during the day under bark, in holes and rock crevices. Lays clutch of 2 eggs.

**Notes:** Those in northern regions have short, thick tails; in south tails are long and slender.

**Status:** Common.

**Similar species:** None.

**HABITAT**
BARK & ROCK
CREVICES

**FOOD**
INSECTS &
LIZARDS

# Shingleback (Lizard)

*Trachydosaurus rugosus* (= wrinkled, rough lizard)

**Length:** HB to 31 cm; T to 8 cm

**Identification:** Large, long-bodied, short-tailed skink with enlarged, rough, pine-cone-like scales on upper surface. Has a huge, triangular (from above) head. Tail short, rounded and blunt-ended. Upper surface pale to dark reddish- or yellowish-brown with paler markings. Underside smooth and pale.

**Where found:** Southern half of Aust., except for eastern and southeastern coastal areas.

**Habits:** Moves slowly across ground during day, feeding on insects, snails, vegetation (including fungi) and carrion⁶. Shelters under timber, grass or ground litter in cold weather. Mates in spring, 2 or 3 large young born in summer.

**Notes:** Tail used to store fat. When threatened, shows blue tongue and hisses, but is reluctant to bite.

**Status:** Secure.

**Similar species:** Bluetongues have smooth scales on backs.

**HABITAT**
WOODLANDS
& PLAINS

**FOOD**
PLANTS &
ANIMALS

# Common Bluetongue

*Tiliqua scincoides* (= *Scincus*-like *tiliqua**)

**Length:** HB to 37 cm; T to 56 cm

**Identification:** Large, long-bodied skink with smooth scales on upper surface. Upper surface pale grey to brown, with 6–9 darker bands across body and 6–8 across tail, which tapers to a point. Underside smooth and pale.

**Where found:** From southeastern SA through Vic., eastern NSW and Qld to northern NT and northwestern WA.

**Habits:** Shelters under timber or litter in colder weather. During day and warm evenings feeds on insects, snails, vegetation and carrion.

Female has live young and may produce up to 25 young at a birth.

**Notes:** One of the world's largest skinks. Blue tongue shown in defensive warning.

**Status:** Secure.

**Similar species:** Centralian Bluetongue, *T. multifasciata*, has 11–13 bands on body; Western Bluetongue, *T. occipitalis*, 5–7.

* After a genus of skinks.

**HABITAT**
FORESTS &
GRASSLANDS

**FOOD**
PLANTS &
ANIMALS

*Varanus gouldii* (= Gould's monitor*)

**Length:** HB to 65.5 cm; T to 100 cm

**Identification:** Very large, ground-living monitor. Upper surface varies from yellow to nearly black, with lighter and darker markings which form crossbands. Dark stripe from eye to ear. Eyes have round pupils, eyelids are well developed. Long forked tongue flicks to carry scent to organ in roof of mouth. Limbs are powerful, digits clawed.

**Where found:** All over Aust. except extreme southeast and in high rainfall forests.

**Habits:** Shelters in a burrow or log. Hunts smaller animals, eats carrion. During breeding season, males may fight. Female buries up to 11 eggs in a nest dug in earth in spring or summer; hatchlings emerge following spring.

**Notes:** Tail used as prop, to balance body, or as weapon.

**Status:** Secure.

**Similar species:** Perentie, *V. giganteus*, is larger, has rows of spots across upper surface.

* Monitors were thought to watch for crocodiles and warn of their presence.

IAN MORRIS

**HABITAT**
GROUND
HABITATS

**FOOD**
CARRION
& GROUND LIFE

# Lace Monitor

*Varanus varius* (= several-coloured monitor)

**Length:** HB to 76.5 cm; T to 134 cm

**Identification:** Large, tree-living monitor which may hunt on ground. Upper surface dark blue with scattered white or yellow scales forming spots and blotches. Black bars across snout, chin and throat. Tail banded with yellow.

**Where found:** Forests, woodlands and plains of eastern coast and ranges; along Murray-Darling River system; Flinders Ranges.

**Habits:** Eats nestling birds as well as other tree-dwelling and ground animals and carrion. Female lays up to 12 eggs in hole in ground or stump or dug into termite mound built in tree or on the ground. She may later return to free the hatchlings (or to dig out nest to lay the following season).

**Notes:** May frequent picnic grounds, hoping for scraps –

is easy to chase away. Takes refuge in tree, keeping on opposite side of trunk from danger.

**Status:** Secure.

**Similar species:** Gould's Goanna *V. gouldii* is ground-dwelling, and its back has yellow background colour rather than dark blue.

HABITAT
WOODLANDS
& PLAINS

FOOD
TREE LIFE
& CARRION

# Southern Angle-headed Dragon

*Hypsilurus spinipes* (= spiny-footed upsilon-tail)

**Length:** HBT to 35 cm

**Identification:** Grey-brown to dark brown above with green and pink blotches. Some have bands across back and tail. Dark band from eye to ear and bars on jaw. Distinct crest of spines along nape and back. Large, wedge-shaped head.

**Where found:** Rainforest and wet eucalypt forest in south-east Qld and north-east NSW.

**Habits:** Lives in trees and is active during the day. Feeds on invertebrates and can be found foraging in leaf littler and along creeks. Lays clutch of 2–7 eggs.

**Notes:** Slow-moving; relies on camouflage when hunting and to escape predators.

**Status:** Common, but habitat declining.

**Similar species:** See Eastern Water Dragon.

 **HABITAT** RAINFOREST & EUCALYPT

**FOOD** INVERTEBRATES

# Eastern Water Dragon

*Physignathus lesueurii* (= Lesueur's puff-cheek)

**Length:** HBT to 65 cm

**Identification:** Grey to grey-brown above with dark bands across back. Cream and blackish rings around tail. Black stripe from eye to neck. Chest flecked red, green or rainbow striped. Mottled yellow-brown below. Crest of spines from nape to end of tail. Tail twice as long as head and body.

**Where found:** Variety of habitats from coastal mangroves to forest and woodland creeks in eastern Aust. Common in urban areas.

**Habits:** Fast-moving, agile tree-climber. Semi-aquatic; it is often seen basking on rocks beside creeks. Feeds on insects, crustaceans, fish, frogs, small reptiles and fruit. Males are territorial. Female lays 1 to 2 clutches of up to 20 eggs in summer. Young hatch in 80 days.

**Habits:** Will leap from trees into water when disturbed.

**Status:** Common.

**Similar species:** See Southern Angle-headed Dragon.

**HABITAT** COASTAL & WOODLANDS

**FOOD** CRUSTACEANS & INSECTS

# Central Bearded Dragon

*Pogona vitticeps* (= banded-headed bearded-lizard)

**Length:** HBT to 55 cm

**Identification:** Large, robust lizard grey to brown above with orange or reddish tinge to body and around eye. Throat pouch has large spines. Distinct row of spines along sides, head and over fore limbs. Juveniles may have blotches or stripes on back.

**Where found:** Woodlands, mallee, hummock grassland and sandplains in arid and semi-arid Australia.

**Habits:** Spends time in trees and shrubs and on the ground.

Active during the day; shelters under logs, leaf litter and spinifex clumps. Feeds on insects and some plants. Female lays two clutches of up to 25 eggs in sloping burrow. Often seen beside roads perched on trees and stumps.

**Notes:** Most active during spring breeding season.

**Status:** Common.

**Similar species:** Bearded Dragon has two rows of oblong patches down its back. Dwarf Bearded Dragon is smaller and has no spines on throat pouch.

IAN MORRIS

**HABITAT**
WOODLANDS & PLAINS

**FOOD**
INSECTS & PLANTS

# Central Netted Dragon

*Ctenophorus nuchalis* (= necked comb-bearer)

**Length:** HBT to 28 cm

**Identification:** Pale reddish-brown above with darker speckling. Pale stripe along back from neck to tail. Pale blotches form bands across head and back. Lower eyelid has fringe of spines. Scattered spines on nape and sides of neck. Head and throat of breeding male tinged orange or red.

**Where found:** In arid regions through central Australia to Western Australia, in open country with red, sandy soils.

**Habits:** Ground-dweller Active during the day and often seen perched above ground on trees, stumps and rocks. Feeds on insects, spiders and soft plants. Lays clutch of 2–6 eggs.

**Notes:** Retreats to shallow burrow at night or when disturbed.

**Status:** Common.

**Similar species:** Several spp. of same family found in region, but are different in size and markings.

**HABITAT**
ARID
COUNTRY

**FOOD**
INSECTS &
SPIDERS

# Frilled Lizard

*Chlamydosaurus kingii* (= King's cloaked lizard)

**Length:** HB to 28 cm; T to 67 cm

**Identification:** A large dragon with a frill of skin around head. Upper surface grey to orange-brown, with darker markings. Frill yellow to black, flashing orange or red when opened. Underside pale; male has black belly. Eye has round pupil and movable lids. Limbs are well developed and digits clawed. If broken off, the tail does not grow again.

**Where found:** In woodlands from Kimberley Division, WA, across top of NT to Cape York Peninsula and eastern Qld.

**Habits:** Perches on tree trunks and on branches, colour and broken outline acting as camouflage<sup>G</sup>. Moves to keep tree between itself and danger. On ground, may run on hindlimbs. Eats insects and other creatures in trees and on ground. Female lays 8–14 eggs.

**Notes:** The reptile emblem of Australia. Frill is supported by rods connected to tongue and jaws, so when mouth opens frill spreads, showing orange and red scales.

**Status:** Not secure.

**Similar species:** None.

**HABITAT**
WARMER
WOODLANDS

**FOOD**
INSECTS &
SMALL LIFE

# Thorny Devil

*Moloch horridus* (= bristly devil)

**Length:** HB to 10 cm; T to 9 cm

**Identification:** Medium-sized dragon with a flattened body, bumpy, spiky skin and a tiny head. Large two-spined hump on neck. Can slowly change colour and pattern to match the ground it stands on.

**Where found:** Dry country, from central coast of WA across interior of Aust., including most of SA, to western Qld.

**Habits:** Moves slowly around in daytime, feeding on small ants (up to 5000 in a meal). Does not drink. Water falling on skin makes its way through series of skin grooves to mouth. Female lays up to 10 eggs in a nest at the end of a long tunnel. Young breed after 3 years, may live to 20 years.

**Notes:** When threatened, bends head so spiky neck bump becomes a false head.

**Status:** Secure.

**Similar species:** None.

**HABITAT**
ARID
COUNTRY

**FOOD**
SMALL
BLACK ANTS

*Pygopus lepidopodus* (= scaly-footed rump-foot)

JIRI LOCHMAN

**Where found:** Usually under vegetation, across southern Aust. from southeastern Qld to Shark Bay, WA.

**Habits:** Hunts spiders and insects on ground during daytime. Grabs and rolls with them to kill them, then laps up body fluids. May lick fruit. Female lays 2 eggs with other females' eggs under rock or log.

**Length:** HB to 27.5 cm; T to 85.5 cm

**Identification:** Large legless lizard with rounded snout and scales on back strongly keeled⁶. Tail more than twice length of head and body. Upper surface grey to tan, striped, spotted or blotched with darker, pale-edged markings. Underside patterned light and dark. Dark bars on lips and sides of neck. Eye without lids, pupil vertical in daylight. No front limb. Large flap instead of hindlimb.

**Notes:** Faces danger by raising head and flattening neck like snake. Tail easily broken off.

**Status:** Secure.

**Similar species:** Hooded Scaly-foot, *P. nigriceps*, whose range is more westerly, hunts at night, has two dark bands across head and neck, sometimes forming hood.

**HABITAT** UNDER LOW VEGETATION

**FOOD** SPIDERS & INSECTS

# Burton's Legless Lizard

*Lialis burtonis* (= *Burton's lialis**)

**Length:** HB to 29 cm; T to 62 cm

**Identification:** Large legless lizard with a long, wedge-shaped head with a sharply pointed snout. Scales on head small and irregular[G]. Colour and pattern very variable; ground colour ranges from cream to black. Scales of upper surface have metallic lustre. Underside coloured and patterned. Eyes with vertical pupil, without lids. No front limb, small triangular hindlimb flap.

**Where found:** On ground under low vegetation in most Aust. habitats except for rainforest, extreme deserts and high mountains.

**Habits:** Active at any time but usually seen hunting in early morning and evening. Waits in hiding for other lizards to pass by, then catches and eats them.

**Notes:** Female (which is larger than male) lays 1, 2 or 3 eggs and may lay more than once in a season, in a nest with other females' eggs.

**Status:** Secure.

**Similar species:** No other legless lizard has a wedge-shaped head.

* Meaning of *lialis* unknown.

JIRI LOCHMAN

**HABITAT**
UNDER LOW
VEGETATION

**FOOD**
OTHER
LIZARDS

# Snakes

## What sort of snake is it?

A key to the families of Australian snakes:

**1** Tail cylinder-shaped, not flattened.....................................**go to 2**

Tail flattened and paddle-shaped .................................**seasnakes**
*(over 30 Australian species)*

**2** Scales on belly more or less equal in size
to scales on back and sides........................................**go to 3**

One row of scales on belly. Each scale at least
three times as wide as a scale on back or sides.........**go to 4**

**3** Eyes well developed. Body scales rough and keeled.
More than 80 scales around middle of body..........**file snakes**
*(2 Australian species)*

Eyes dark spots beneath scales. Body scales smooth.
Fewer than 40 scales around middle of body......**blind snakes**
*(over 40 Australian species)*

**4** Fewer than 30 scales around middle of body.................**go to 5**

More than 30 scales around middle of body................**pythons**
*(15 Australian species)*

**5** Two scales cover vent .............................................**colubrid snakes**
*(11 Australian species)*

Single scale covers vent .........................................**elapid snakes**
*(75 Australian species)*

*Acrochordus arafurae* (= Arafura* pointed-scale)

**Length** HDT
to 164 cm

**Identification:**
Large, water-living snake with small head and loose skin. Upper surface grey to dark brown, marked with pale blotches. Scales small, keeled and resemble teeth of file. Tail is prehensile[G].

STANLEY BREEDEN

**Where found:** Coastal wetlands in northern Aust.

**Habits:** Can move on land but seldom leaves water. Spends day in shaded water, hunts at night. Anchors itself by its tail, then ambushes passing fish. Lacks venom, so holds prey with help of rough scales and long curved teeth. Several males court a female, who later produces up to 27 young.

**Notes:** Breathes through nostrils pushed above water, and also through the skin. May move into flooded grassland during Wet season. Harmless to humans.

**Status:** Secure.

**Similar species:** Little File Snake, *A. granulatus*, smaller, marked with narrow bands.

* The Arafura Sea bounds the northern coast of Australia.

**HABITAT**
NORTHERN
WETLANDS

**FOOD**
FISH

# Black-headed Python

*Aspidites melanocephalus* (= black-headed shield-bearer)

STANLEY BREEDEN

**Length:** HB to 265 cm; T to 35 cm

**Identification:** A large, small-headed, round-snouted python with a glossy black head and neck. Upper surface of body and tail light tan to brown, with many darker cross bands. Eye has vertical pupil. Lips lack heat-sensing pits present in most other pythons.

**Where found:** Plains and ranges across northern half of Aust.

**Habits:** Ground-living python which shelters in cracks in soil, burrows, fallen trees, termite mounds and caves. At night, hunts for ground-living birds, mammals and reptiles, including snakes. Lacks venom and kills prey by crushing it in body coils. Males fight in mating season. Female lays 5–9 eggs, coils round them and may warm them by shivering.

**Notes:** During cool weather, black head is pushed into sunlight and warms rapidly.

**Status:** Secure.

**Similar species:** Woma Python, *A. ramsayi*, of drier central Aust., the other python without lip pits, lacks black head colour.

**HABITAT** PLAINS & RANGES

**FOOD** REPTILES & OTHER LIFE

# Diamond (Carpet) Python

*Morelia spilota* (= spotted *Morelia*)

**Length:** HB to 350 cm; T to 50 cm

**Identification:** Diamond Python subspecies[G] has upper surface green-black, with cream or yellow spots forming diamond pattern (see right). Carpet Python subspecies has upper surface pale to dark brown, with paler blotches, each with dark border forming "carpet" pattern (see below).

**Where found:** Aust. except southern Vic., arid Centre and northwest.

**Habits:** Often hunts and shelters in trees, but may hunt on ground and shelter in

burrows of other animals. Eats birds and mammals, killing them by crushing them with its body. Female lays up to 50 eggs, then coils around them until they hatch.

**Notes:** Tracks prey using heat-sensitive pits on lips. Has no venom and is harmless to humans. Kills rats, mice.

**Status:** Secure.

**Similar snakes:** There are 3 subspecies of this python and numbers of other colour forms.

**HABITAT** TREES & GROUND

**FOOD** BIRDS & MAMMALS

# 🐍 Blackish Blind Snake

*Rhamphotyphlops nigrescens* (= blackish beaked blind-eye)

**Length:** HBT to 75 cm

**Identification:** Wormlike burrowing snake with shiny scales (same size all around body). Eyes are small spots. Small mouth behind and below snout. Upper surface purplish to blackish. Underside cream or pinkish. Very short tail ends in a spine.

IAN MORRIS

**Where found:** On or in ground in forests, woodlands and plains, in eastern Aust. from southern Qld to Vic.

**Habits:** On surface of ground only on warm nights, usually after rain. Shelters under rocks, in soil under leaf litter or in deserted termite mounds, sometimes with others of its kind. Eats eggs, larvae and pupae of ants, as well as worms and leeches. Female lays 5–20 eggs in mid to late summer.

**Notes:** Body suited to burrowing. Glossy scales overlap and head and neck produce oily substance which eases passage through soil. When threatened, may curl with head hidden and lift up tail. Blind snakes are non-venomous and harmless to humans.

**Status:** Secure.

**Similar species:** This is the largest blind snake.

**HABITAT**
IN SOIL,
UNDER LITTER

**FOOD**
YOUNG OF
ANTS; WORMS

144

# Green Tree Snake

*Dendrelaphis punctulata* (= fine-spotted tree-snake)

**Length:** HB 1 to 170 cm

**Identification:** Slender, tree-living snake with large eyes. Varies greatly in colour, upper surface from pale green to grey-blue to nearly black. Skin between scales is pale blue. Underside may be yellow, lime green or pale blue. Keeled belly scales give a good grip on branches, helped by long, whip-like, prehensile tail.

**Where found:** Forests, heaths and woodlands, in coastal northern and eastern Aust.

**Habits:** Lives in trees and other vegetation, shelters in tree hollows, under rocks, in caves and sometimes in buildings. Hunts during day and evening, taking frogs and lizards. Has no venom and is harmless to humans.

**Notes:** When threatened, lifts the head and flattens the neck sideways, showing blue skin between the scales.

**Status:** Secure.

**Similar species:** Northern Tree-snake, *D. calligastra*, has dark streak along side of head and larger eye, is found only in northeastern Qld.

JIRI LOCHMAN

**HABITAT**
FORESTS &
WOODLANDS

**FOOD**
FROGS &
REPTILES

# Dugite

*Pseudonaja affinis* (= related false-cobra)

**Length:** HBT to 200 cm

**Identification:** Medium to large, fast-moving brown snake with small head. Upper surface brown or brownish grey with black spots. Underside pale grey or brown, with darker blotches. Blackish brown iris, gold rim around pupil. Inside of mouth pink.

**Where found:** Area around coast of southwestern WA.

**Habits:** Ground-living snake which is active by day, hunting mammals, lizards and snakes. Alert and nervous, if it feels threatened it rears its forebody, hisses and strikes. In breeding season, males wrestle in combat. Female lays up to 31 eggs in burrow or under rock.

**Notes:** Dugite and related "brown snakes" have powerful venom, which can be fatal to humans. If bitten, apply elastic bandage to limb and seek immediate medical attention. Antivenom[G] is available.

**Status:** Secure.

**Similar species:** Gwardar, *P. nuchalis*, in dry regions to north and east of Dugite. Eastern Brown Snake, *P. textilis*, in eastern, less dry areas of Aust. Bite from either is potentially fatal.

MARIE LOCHMAN

**HABITAT**
SANDPLAIN & HEATH

**FOOD**
MAMMALS & REPTILES

146

# Coastal Taipan

*Oxyuranus scutellatus* (= small-shielded sharp-tail)

**Length:**
HBT 2 – 3 m.

**Identification:**
Light to dark brown above; head or snout can be pale yellowish-cream. Sides cream-brown; belly cream to yellow with orange flecks. Head coffin-shaped and distinct from body. Reddish-brown eyes.

**Where found:** Northern and NE Australia to Qld/NSW border in eucalypt forests, grassy woodland, canefields.

**Habits:** Most active during day and at dusk. Feeds on rodents and other small animals. Shelters in burrows and thick vegetation. Males engage in ritual combat.

Female lays 3–20 eggs.

**Notes:** Fast and alert. Aggressive when threatened. Venomous.

**Status:** Common but rarely seen.

**Similar species:** King Brown Snake has heavier body and division between head and body is less obvious.

**HABITAT** FORESTS & WOODLANDS

**FOOD** SMALL MAMMALS

# Northern Death Adder

*Acanthophis praelongus* (= very long spine-snake*)

IAN MORRIS

**Length:** HBT to 70 cm

**Identification:** Ground-living snake with large head, narrow neck and strong body. Upper surface dark brown to reddish brown, with paler cross-bands. Head scales are rough and form brow-ridges over eyes. Pupil is vertical in daylight. Tail tapers sharply and end bears a spine.

**Where found:** On loose soil or under leaf litter, in woodland or grassland across northern Aust.

**Habits:** Shelters under ground litter in shade of rocks or trees during day. Camouflaged by colour, stillness, lies in wait for lizards, frogs, birds and mammals. End of the tail is held near head and acts as a lure to bring prey close.

**Notes:** Fangs are long and venom is powerful. Warns by flattening body and flicking forebody from side to side. Bite is potentially fatal to humans and requires immediate medical attention.

**Status:** Probably secure.

**Similar species:** Southern Death Adder, *A. antarcticus*, in south and southeast of Aust., Desert Death Adder, *A. pyrrhus*, in northwest and Centre.

* Refers to spine at end of tail.

**HABITAT**
WOODLAND,
GRASSLAND

**FOOD**
REPTILES,
FROGS

# Eastern Tiger Snake

*Notechis scutatus* (= shielded southern snake)

**Length:** HBT to 210 cm

**Identification:** Large snake with broad, strong body. Upper surface brown, brown-green or blackish with pale bands. Underside cream, yellow or grey.

**Where found:** In damp, cool habitats such as swamps, and woodlands on coastal lowlands and plains of southeastern Aust., from southeastern Qld to southeastern SA, and Murray River valley.

**Habits:** Ground-living snake which is active by day and during warm evenings, hunting frogs, reptiles, nestling birds and fish. Shelters in burrows, in logs and under timber. If threatened, curves the forebody off the ground, flattening it, and hisses loudly. Adult males wrestle. Female has up to 80 live young.

**Notes:** Shy, but bites if threatened. Venom of this and other related tiger snakes is potentially fatal to humans. Antivenom is available.

**Status:** Secure.

**Similar species:** Subspecies known as Western Tiger Snake, *N. s. occidentalis*, occurs in southwestern WA.

**HABITAT** SWAMPS, WOODLANDS

**FOOD** FROGS & REPTILES

# Copperhead

*Austrelaps superbus* (= superb southern-*Elaps*)

**Length:** HBT to 1.7 m

**Identification:** Heavy-bodied snake with narrow head. Ranges from reddish-brown to grey to black above. Sides cream, yellow or red; belly cream. Pale bars on lips and side of head. Young may have dark bands across neck and back.

**Where found:** Near marshes and swamps in SE Australia between NSW and SA borders; Tasmania.

**Habits:** Active day and night. Congregates in large groups. Feeds on lizards, snakes, frogs and small mammals. Mate in spring; average clutch size of 17 eggs.

**Notes:** Unlike most snakes remains active in cooler weather. Venomous but not aggressive.

**Similar species:** Two subspecies have different range or habitat.

 **HABITAT** SWAMPS & MARSHES

 **FOOD** FROGS & SMALL MAMMALS

# Red-bellied Black Snake

*Pseudechis porphyriacus* (= purple false viper)

**Length:**
HT to 2 m

**Identification:** Glossy black above; snout can be light brown. Sides bright red or pink dulling towards belly. Underside of tail is black.

**Where found:** Near streams, swamps in wetter parts of eastern and south-eastern Australia.

**Habits:** Active during the day. Feeds mainly on frogs; also eats lizards, small mammals and birds. Congregates in spring when males engage in ritual combat. Female bears 8–40 live young in membranous sacs.

**Notes:** Numbers decreasing in Qld because of predation on poisonous Cane Toad. May take up strike pose when threatened. Venomous.

**Status:** Common.

**Similar species:** Small-eyed Snake, *Rhinoplocephalus nigrescens*, smaller and pink belly does not extend up sides.

**HABITAT**
STREAMS &
SWAMPS

**FOOD**
FROGS, BIRDS
MAMMALS

# ⌇ Yellow-faced Whipsnake

*Demansia psammophis* (= Van Diemen's sand-snake)

**Length:** HBT to 110 cm

**Identification:** A slender-bodied, thin-necked, fast-moving snake. Upper surface varies in colour from light grey to reddish, each scale edged darker. Under surface grey to cream. Each large eye is rimmed dark, and forms the head of a "comma" whose tail is a dark marking, bordered yellow, which slants back towards the angle of the mouth.

**Where found:** In many habitats over most of Aust., except for tropical north from Kimberley Division, WA, to western Qld.

**Habits:** A day hunter, feeding on small lizards, frogs and reptile eggs. Female lays up to 9 eggs, sometimes in a nest with other females' eggs. It is venomous, though reluctant to bite. Only a very large individual is likely to harm a human, but if bitten seek medical advice.

**Notes:** Up to 20 adults have been found together in a refuge in cold winter weather.

**Status:** Common.

**Similar species:** None.

JIRI LOCHMAN

**HABITAT**
WOODLAND & PLAINS

**FOOD**
FROGS & LIZARDS

# Stephens's Banded Snake

*Hoplocephalus stephensii* (= Stephens's armoured-head)

**Length:** HBT to 125 cm

**Identification:** Broad-headed, slender-bodied, climbing snake. Upper surface black, with bright yellow scales forming cross-bands two or more scales in width. Yellow spots on head, yellow bars on upper lip. Underside grey, with keeled scales.

**Where found:** Wooded ranges and rainforest edges, from Gosford, NSW, to southern Qld.

**Habits:** Lives and shelters in trees. Hunts lizards, small mammals (bats) and birds in tree hollows and crevices in rocks. Female has 2–12 young every second year.

**Notes:** This snake shelters in scars in tree trunks which only become suitable when tree is mature. Selective timber felling destroys habitat. Bite requires medical assessment.

**Status:** Rare and endangered.

**Similar species:** Endangered Broad-headed Snake, *H. bungaroides*, of Sydney area.

**HABITAT** MATURE TREES

**FOOD** REPTILES & MAMMALS

# Wide-faced Sea Krait

*Laticauda colubrina* (= serpent-like flat-tail)

**Length:** HT to 1.4 m

**Identification:** Black and bluish-grey bands extend around belly. Pale yellow snout, upper lip and neck band. Nostrils on side of rounded head.

**Where found:** Coastal NE Aust., especially Torres Strait.

**Habits:** Partly terrestrial. Feeds on gobies and other small fish. Female lays clutch of 4–20 eggs on land. Most active at night; will forage on reefs and in mangroves during the day.

**Notes:** Venomous.

**Status:** Common but only seen occasionally.

**Similar species:** *L. laticaudata* has yellow bar over eye, upper lip is brown and bands do not extend around belly.

IAN MORRIS

**HABITAT** COASTAL

**FOOD** GOBIES & FISH

# Golden Seasnake

*Aipysurus laevis* (= smooth high-tail)

**Length:**
HBT to 170 cm

**Identification:**
Large, strong-necked, thick-bodied seasnake with paddle-like tail. Upper surface has smooth scales, and varies in colour from dark purple- or green-brown to cream.

May have lighter or darker spots on body. Underside has keeled scales and is paler in colour.

**Where found:** Around tropical coasts and reefs off northern Aust.

**Habits:** Shelters among or near coral, is active day or night. An individual may be found regularly in one part of a reef. Hunts by probing crevices amongst corals for sleeping fish, prawns, crabs and fish eggs. Female gives birth to 1–5 large young.

**Notes:** The seasnake most likely to be seen by divers. Will investigate swimmer closely, then swim away. Not usually aggressive. Venom is powerful and potentially fatal to humans. Seek medical assistance if bitten.

**Status:** Secure.

**Similar species:** None.

**HABITAT**
CORAL REEFS
AND COASTS

**FOOD**
FISH &
MARINE LIFE

# Frogs

An animal is a frog if it:

- 🐾 has a backbone and skull
- 🐾 is cold-blooded
- 🐾 has moist skin with glands
- 🐾 lays eggs in water or damp places
- 🐾 changes shape during its life cycle

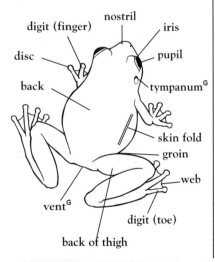

## A frog's life cycle

- 🐾 A tadpole has gills, a tail and no legs.
- 🐾 An adult frog has lungs, four legs and no tail.

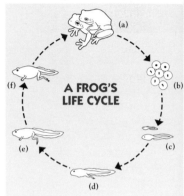

A FROG'S LIFE CYCLE

(a) Adult frogs mate

(b) Eggs hatch

(c) Tadpoles grow

(d) Hind legs develop

(e) Front leg emerges

(f) Other front leg emerges. Then the tail is absorbed, the lungs develop and finally the frog leaves the water

## Where and when

Damp places, such as forest leaf-litter and the edges of creeks and ponds are the best places to look for frogs. They shelter during the day and are most active at night when searching for food. The best time to look for frogs is during or after heavy rain, especially in warm weather, for this is the time when frogs look for mates.

# Frog groups

Frogs are the only group of amphibians native to Australia. They are divided into four families.

*Tree-frogs* and related species usually have feet with special features to suit their lifestyle, such as sticky discs for climbing or hard-edged inner toes for digging. Their eggs are laid in water.

| Hylidae | tree-frogs, burrowing frogs |

*Narrow-mouthed frogs* are found in rainforests and monsoon forests of northern Australia. The eggs are laid on land and usually guarded by a parent. These tiny frogs hatch fully-formed.

| Microhylidae | Fry's Chirper |

*Southern frogs* are found throughout Australia. They tend to be heavy bodied burrowers or ground-dwellers. Some lay eggs in water, others on land. Life cycles vary with some species having no tadpole stage.

| Myobatrachidae | froglets, burrowing frogs, banjo frogs |

*True frogs* have two vocal sacs. There is only one species in Australia but they are common in the northern hemisphere.

| Ranidae | bullfrogs |

There are no native toads (Bufonidae) in Australia. The Cane Toad was introduced in 1935.

# Green Tree-frog

*Litoria caerulea* (= blue* beach-frog)

**Length:** ♀ 6–11; ♂ 6.6–7.7 cm

**Identification:** Large (cricket-ball-sized) tree-frog with smooth green to green-brown skin on back and sides, sometimes spotted white. Underside is white, with coarsely grainy texture. Back of thigh is yellow to maroon. Pupil horizontal[G], iris pale yellow to gold. Large glands on back of head. Fold of skin overhangs tympanum. Digits end in large discs. Fingers are ¹/₃ webbed, toes ³/₄ webbed.

**Where found:** Across northern half of Aust. In moist, cool places, in both natural situations and human constructions such as toilets and drainpipes.

**Call:** Deep, repeated *crawk...crawk.*

**Habits:** Spends daytime in moist refuge, hunts small creatures at night. Active climber. Lays 200–2000 eggs after rain falls (Nov.–Feb.). Mottled brown or green tadpoles grow 4.5–10.0 cm, take about 6 weeks to mature to frogs.

**Notes:** Becomes very used to humans. If removed from refuge tends to return. Less active in cold, dry weather, begins calling when rain falls.

**Status[G]:** Secure.

**Similar species:** Magnificent Tree-frog, *L. splendida*, has gland covering entire head. White-lipped Tree-frog, *L. infrafrenata*, has white stripe around edge of lower jaw.

* Named after a dead frog preserved in alcohol, which turned it blue.

**HABITAT**
MOIST
PLACES

**FOOD**
INSECTS &
SMALL LIFE

# Red-eyed Green Tree-frog

*Litoria chloris* (= green beach-frog)

**Length:** ♀ 5.8–6.8; ♂ 5.4–6.2 cm

**Identification:** Medium (tennis-ball-sized) tree-frog with smooth, bright green back and white to bright yellow, grainy underside. Back of thigh is purple or brown. Pupil is horizontal, iris is gold in centre, orange or red at edge. Digits end in large discs. Fingers are ³/₄ webbed, toes are ⁷/₈ webbed.

**Where found:** Coastal wet forests and regrowth around clearings, along northern NSW coast and Qld coast, as far north as Proserpine.

**Call:** Repeated, long, moaning *aaa-rk...aaa-rk*, followed by soft trill.

**Habits:** Lives in foliage high in trees. After heavy rain, usually Oct.–Feb., calls from lower branches. Large groups gather around flooded areas and overflow ponds to breed. Eggs laid singly or in clumps in shallow water. Pale brown tadpoles grow to 7.4 cm.

**Notes:** Because of their treetop habitat, these frogs are usually seen only after heavy rain falls and they come to the ground to breed.

**Status:** Secure.

**Similar species:** Orange-thighed Frog, *L. xanthomera*, found north of Proserpine, Qld, has orange at back of thigh.

IAN MORRIS

**HABITAT**
COASTAL
FORESTS

**FOOD**
INSECTS &
SMALL LIFE

# Naked (Red) Tree-frog

*Litoria rubella* (= red beach-frog)

**Length:** ♀ 3.4–4.3; ♂ 2.8–3.7 cm

**Identification:** Small (ping-pong-ball-sized) stocky tree-frog with smooth, pale grey to reddish-brown back, with small darker flecks. Dark stripe along side of head and body. Underside is white and grainy (throat of breeding male is dark grey). Groin is yellow. Pupil is horizontal, iris is gold. Limbs are short; digits have large discs; fingers are slightly webbed, toes ²/₃ webbed.

**Call:** Long, pulsing note, rising towards end.

**Where found:** Northern ³/₄ of Aust. Absent from southern coastal areas.

**Habits:** Spends day sheltering under stone or bark, sometimes in a building or under a water pipe. Breeds straight after heavy rain. Males call from ground near water. Thin layer of up to 300 eggs floats on surface. Tadpole is pale brown and grows to 3.9 cm.

**Notes:** Found in both arid and wet coastal areas. Breeding time varies according to rain.

**Status:** Secure.

**Similar species:** Buzzing Tree-frog, *L. electrica*, around Gulf of Carpentaria. Bleating Tree-frog, *L. dentata*, in coastal southern Qld and northern to central NSW. Both have large, dark markings on their backs.

JIRI LOCHMAN

**HABITAT**
PLAINS &
FORESTS

**FOOD**
INSECTS &
SMALL LIFE

# Blue Mountains Tree-frog

*Litoria citropa* (= lemon-coloured beach-frog)

**Length:** ♀ 5.6–5.7; ♂ 4.7–5.7 cm

**Identification:** Medium-sized tree-frog. Smooth skin on the top of the head and back is light to dark brown, flecked or mottled black. Green on side of head, on flank and on limbs. Black line from nostril through eye over tympanum to groin. Side, groin, inner and outer thigh are orange-red. Pupil is horizontal, iris is gold. Digits have large discs. Fingers lack webbing, toes are half-webbed.

**Call:** A scream, followed by a soft trill.

**Where found:** Flowing streams in rocky, forested areas, from the Great Dividing Range to the coast in NSW and eastern Vic.

**Habits:** Rarely seen unless the determined frog-watcher searches the preferred habitat of rocky outcrops. Males call in Sept. and Oct., usually from near fast-flowing water.

Eggs may be found on rocks or in pools in streams. Tadpole is dark brown marked with gold, grows to 3.4 cm.

**Notes:** Described as Australia's most beautiful frog, and featured on a postage stamp.

**Status:** Secure.

**Similar species:** None.

IAN MORRIS

**HABITAT**
STREAMS,
FORESTS

**FOOD**
INSECTS &
SMALL LIFE

161

# Striped Rocket-frog

*Litoria nasuta* (= large-nosed beach-frog)

**Length:** ♀ 3.6–5.5; ♂ 3.3–4.5 cm

**Identification:** Medium-sized, streamlined frog with a long snout, long arms and very long, powerful legs. Centre of back pale brown, bordered by darker brown areas, marked with still darker bumps. Skin folds run down back. Black and white stripes from nose along side to flank. Underside is white and grainy. Back of thigh is yellow with dark brown stripes. Tympanum has white border. Discs on digits are small. No webs between fingers.

**Call:** *Wick–wick–wick…but… but…but.*

**Where found:** Coastal waterways and swamps, from north of Newcastle, NSW, to Cape York Peninsula, and across NT to Kimberley, WA.

**Habits:** Lives on ground, hunts at night. Breeds between Nov. and Feb. in northern Aust. Groups of 50–100 eggs float on surface of water. Tadpoles are mottled with brown above and may grow to 5.6 cm.

**Notes:** This frog is a fast, strong leaper.

**Status:** Secure.

**Similar species:** Freycinet's Frog, *L. freycineti*, found in northeastern NSW and southwest Qld, also has long hindlegs, but has rows of warts rather than narrow skin folds on its back.

**HABITAT**
SWAMPS &
WATERWAYS

**FOOD**
INSECTS &
SMALL LIFE

# Water-holding Frog

*Cyclorana platycephala* (= flat-headed round-frog)

**Length:** ♀ 5.0–7.2;
♂ 4.2–6.4 cm

**Identification:** Medium-sized, round-bodied, short-legged frog. Dull grey, brown or green back, sometimes marked with pale stripe down centre and darker patches. Head flattened, and tympanum much larger than eye. Small eye set high on head, has horizontal pupil, gold iris. No webs on fingers, but toes are fully webbed. Shovel-shaped tubercle⁶ on inner side of foot.

PETER SLATER

**Call:** Repeated, lengthy *maw-w..maw-w-w.*

**Where found:** Inland arid areas of all Aust. except Vic., near waterholes and swamps which fill after rain.

**Habits:** In dry conditions, uses sharp-edged tubercle on foot to dig burrow at foot of bush or tree and aestivates⁶. Frog's outer layer of skin forms a water-saving cocoon, its bladder serves as storage tank for water in form of very dilute urine. After rain falls, frog surfaces, sheds and eats cocoon, feeds and breeds.

**Notes:** Two separated groups (see map). Can capture food in water, and webbed feet make it a good swimmer. Used as water source by humans.

**Status:** Secure.

**Similar species:** No other burrowing frog has a flattened head, small eyes, no eye-stripe and fully webbed toes.

**HABITAT**
INLAND
ARID AREAS

**FOOD**
INSECTS &
SMALL LIFE

# Northern Snapping (Giant) Frog

*Cyclorana australis* (= southern round-frog)

IAN MORRIS

**Length:** ♀ 7.1–10.5; ♂ 7.1–7.9 cm

**Identification:** A large, burrowing frog with a large, flattish, broad head and very large eyes. Skin of back bumpy and may be pale brown, grey or green, with dark markings or green patches. Broad, dark stripe from tip of nose to flank. One skin fold runs down each side of the backbone, another on each side to the flank. Pupil is horizontal, iris gold. Back of thigh is patterned. Fingers are unwebbed, toes have small webs. A shovel-shaped tubercle on inner side of foot.

**Call:** Short, repeated *unk…unk…unk.*

**Where found:** Open forest and grassland across northern Australia, from Broome to western side of the base of Cape York Peninsula.

**Habits:** Often seen during the Wet season, sometimes basking in hot sunshine beside water. During Dry remains in burrow. Breeds in Wet, between Dec. and Feb., laying up to 7000 eggs in temporary water. Creamy gold tadpoles grow to 7.0 cm and swim in large groups.

**Notes:** Has a tremendous gape[G] and will eat any creature small enough to swallow, including other frogs.

**Status:** Secure.

**Similar species:** New Holland Frog, *C. novaehollandiae,* which lacks the pattern on the back of the thigh, replaces this frog in most of Queensland.

**HABITAT**
FLOODED
GRASSLAND

**FOOD**
INSECTS &
SMALL LIFE

# Tusked Frog

*Adelotus brevis* (= short unseen frog)

**Length:** ♀ 2.9–3.8,
♂ 3.4–3.8 mm

**Identification:** Small,
large-headed, flattened
frog. Skin on back is
rough with warts and
ridges, and is grey or
brown, patterned
darker. Throat grey
with white flecks, belly
smooth and black with
white spots (males)
or marbling (females).
Both sexes have tusk-
like teeth at front of lower jaw.
Bright red patches in groin and
on back of hindleg.

IAN MORRIS

**Call:** *Kuruk*, repeated several
times a minute.

**Where found:** In forest and
open country, on the coastal
plain and in the Great
Dividing Range, from central
eastern Qld to southern NSW.

**Habits:** Lives under rocks or
logs, or in crevices, near water.
Pale cream eggs are laid in a
foam nest, usually away from
direct light. Male remains with
nest until tadpoles hatch.

**Notes:** Male is larger than
female (not usual in frogs) and
male head is wider than (and
may be same size as) its body.
The tusks are used in fights
between males.

**Status:** Secure.

**Similar species:** No other
frog has such a large head
and tusks.

**HABITAT**
FORESTS &
PLAINS

**FOOD**
INSECTS &
SMALL LIFE

# Southern Gastric-brooding Frog

*Rheobatrachus silus* (= pug-nosed stream-frog)

**Length:** ♀ 4.5–5.4; ♂ 3.3–4.1 cm

**Identification:** Medium-sized, water-dwelling, short-snouted frog with slimy skin and large, powerful hindlegs. Bumpy back varies from brown to greenish, with darker patches. Underside white with patches of yellow. The large eyes, which have vertical[G] pupils, are set on top of the head. Fingers are unwebbed, toes fully webbed.

**Call:** A rising note.

**Where found:** In rocky rainforest streams and pools above 300 m altitude[G], in the Conondale and Blackall Ranges, southeastern Qld.

**Habits:** Lives in water, and is active at night. A female swallows up to 25 fertilised eggs (or possibly tadpoles), which develop to adult frogs in her stomach. After around 6 weeks, small frogs emerge from their mother's mouth; she then begins feeding again.

**Notes:** May be seen drifting in water, or floating on its back. Tongue cannot be flicked out of mouth, so probably gulps insects from water. This remarkable frog has not been seen since 1981.

**Status:** May be extinct.

**Similar species:** Larger (♀ 6.6–7.9 mm) Northern Gastric-brooding Frog, *R. vitellinus*, of Clarke Range, near Mackay, Qld, not seen since 1985.

OWEN KELLY

**HABITAT**
RAINFOREST
STREAMS

**FOOD**
INSECTS &
WATER LIFE

# Desert Spadefoot Frog

*Notaden nichollsi* (= Nicholls's back-gland*)

**Length:** ♀ 4.6–6.5; ♂ 4.2–5.8 cm

**Identification:** Small, fat, short-legged frog with a short head and bumpy skin. The back is green-grey to brown, spotted with yellow and red warts, while the underside is pale. The tympanum is not obvious. The eye has a horizontal pupil. The fingers are unwebbed, the toes are slightly webbed.

IAN MORRIS

**Call:** A loud *woop…woop…woop.*

**Where found:** In aridland and grassland, from northwestern WA across to southwestern Qld and south to northern SA.

**Habits:** During drought aestivates at end of burrow sunk up to 2 m into ground. With rain, comes to surface, feeds on ants and termites.

Males call while floating in water. Up to 1000 eggs laid in a chain in flooded vegetation. Pale brown tadpoles may become frogs in only 16 days.

**Notes:** One of four *Notaden* species which can survive long dry periods in their burrow then breed in temporary flooding after rain falls. Runs rather than hops.

**Status:** Secure.

**Similar species:** No other *Notaden* species in its range.

* *Notaden* frogs have skin glands which "sweat" a distasteful substance.

**HABITAT**
ARID
COUNTRY

**FOOD**
ANTS &
TERMITES

# Western Spotted Frog

*Heleioporus albopunctatus* (= white-spotted marsh-dweller)

JIRI LOCHMAN

**Length:** ♀ 6.0–8.5; ♂ 5.6–7.7 cm

**Identification:** Large, fat, burrowing frog, with a broad, rounded head. Back and sides are leather-textured and dark brown to black, spotted with white or yellow. The underside is white. A white stripe runs from front of eye to snout and another from bottom of eye to hinge of mouth. The pupil is vertical. Digits are unwebbed, toes short. Foot has a large digging tubercle on its inner side. Breeding male has black spines on the first finger.

**Call:** Repeated short, high *coo…coo*.

**Where found:** In sandy country, usually near water, in the southwest of WA, except southwestern corner.

**Habits:** Males call from the mouths of their burrows, females search them out. 250–700 eggs are deposited and fertilised to form a frothy mass. Hatching takes place after the burrow is flooded by rain.

**Notes:** Seen on the surface on summer and autumn nights. Calling begins with winter rains in April or May. To locate a calling male, find the entrance to his burrow.

**Status:** Not common.

**Similar species:** Other *Heleioporus* species found in southwestern WA lack white or yellow spots on the back.

**HABITAT**
SANDY
SWAMPS

**FOOD**
INSECTS &
SMALL LIFE

# Moaning Frog

*Heleioporus eyrei* (= Eyre's marsh-dweller)

**Size:**
♂ 4.5 – 6.55 cm
♀ 4.5–6.5 cm

**Identification:**
Medium-sized, stout frog with broad, rounded head. Brown to dark grey above with white, yellow or pale grey patches on back and sides. White below; brown on throat. Long fifth toe on hind limbs. No webbing between fingers.

DARRAN LEAL

**Call:** Long, low moan repeated slowly.

**Where found:** High rainfall areas of south-west WA and on Rottnest Island. Coastal swamps with sandy soil.

**Habits:** Breeds April–June. Male calls from burrow entrance. Female lays frothy mass of 80–500 eggs in burrow. Tadpoles hatch after burrow floods.

**Notes:** Tadpoles are mottled black and gold with red stripe down back.

**Status:** Secure.

**Similar species:** Plains Frog, *H. inornatus*, and Sand Frog, *H. psammophilus*, have different calls.

**HABITAT**
SANDY
SWAMPS

**FOOD**
INSECTS

# Ornate Burrowing Frog

*Limnodynastes ornatus* (= decorated lord-of-marsh)

**Size:** ♂ 3.5–4.2 cm
♀ 2.9–3.7 cm

**Identification:** Small frog with broad, angular head. Varies from dark grey or brown above to pale grey or brown with darker patterns; often with a light patch on head behind eyes and dark band between eyes. Dark bars on upper lip and limbs. White below. Horizontal pupil. No webbing on fingers; toes one-quarter webbed.

**Call:** *unk...unk*, repeated slowly.

**Where found:** Near permanent and semi-permanent water in all habitats from desert to rainforest in northern and eastern Australia.

**Habits:** Feeds on insects. Burrows but becomes active after rain or on warm, humid nights. Congregates at waterholes after heavy rain to breed. A female lays up to 1600 eggs laid in a foamy mass. Tadpoles complete development in 3 weeks.

**Notes:** Dormant in dry season. Tadpoles are pale brown.

**Status:** Secure.

**Similar species:** Spencer's Burrowing Frog, *L. spenceri*, has more webbing on toes and a haw...haw...haw call.

**HABITAT** GRASS LANDS

**FOOD** ANTS & TERMITES

# Northern Banjo Frog

*Limnodynastes terraereginae* (= Queensland lord-of-the-marshes)

**Length:** ♀ 5.5–7.9; ♂ 6.0–7.6 cm

**Identification:** A large, burrowing frog. The bumpy skin of the back is brown or black, with darker markings and a paler central stripe. The underside is cream, the side yellow with black markings, the groin yellow and scarlet. The male displays a yellow throat sac. A yellow gland runs from beneath the eye back to the shoulder. Horizontal pupil, gold iris. Digits have no discs. Toes have small webs.

**Call:** Repeated *plonk…plonk… plonk* like plucking a banjo.

**Where found:** Vegetation near still water, in woodlands and forests in coastal eastern Aust. Some inland range in NSW.

**Habits:** Found near permanent water. Hides in grass or other vegetation during day. After rain, from Oct. to May, breeding males call from water. Tadpoles reach 6.5 cm, have dark bodies and mottled tails.

**Notes:** As female lays eggs, she paddles with her broad inner fingers. Air bubbles pass under her body, mingle with the eggs and jelly coming from her vent and form a floating foam nest.

**Status:** Secure.

**Similar species:** Pobblebonk, *L. dorsalis*, in southwestern WA. Giant Bullfrog, *L. interioris*, of drier areas NSW and Vic. lacks scarlet in groin.

**HABITAT** PLANTS NEAR WATER

**FOOD** INSECTS & SMALL LIFE

# Corroboree Frog

*Pseudophryne corroboree* (= corroboree false toad)

**Size:** ♂ 2.6–3 cm
♀ 2.6–2.8 cm

**Identification:** Distinctive shiny-skinned frog. Bright yellow and black or lime green and black stripes and narrow blotches.

**Call:** Grating *ark...ark*.

**Where found:** Australian Alps in NSW to ACT border in grassy marshland above tree line and edges of woodlands.

**Habits:** Feeds on ants and mites. Breeds Jan–March. 10–30 large eggs laid in burrow made in sphagnum moss, grass or sedges. Male stays with eggs. Tadpoles take 30 weeks to develop into frogs before hatching.

**Notes:** Green colour form occurs in northern part of range.

**Status:** Vulnerable to habitat loss through bushfires.

**Similar species:** None.

 **HABITAT** MARSHLAND & WOODLAND

 **FOOD** ANTS & MITES

# Fry's Chirper

*Sphenophryne fryi* (= Fry's wedge-shaped toad)

**Size:**
♂ 2.3–3.5 cm
♀ 2.3–2.4 cm

IAN MORRIS

**Identification:**
Small frog with smooth skin. Above greyish-brown head blending to reddish brown over back and legs; dark speckles may be present. Sides of head darker than top. Distinct black or dark brown stripe on sides of head. Orange below with light dots. No webbing on toes or fingers.

**Call:** series of brief whistle-like notes.

**Where found:** Rainforest from Cairns to Cooktown.

**Habits:** Lives under logs and leaf litter on forest floor. Lays 7–12 eggs on damp soil under debris. An adult usually tends eggs. Tadpoles metamorphose in eggs.

**Notes:** One of only 5 spp. of this genus found in Australia.

**Status:** Vulnerable to loss of habitat.

**Similar species:** Rain Frog, *S. pluvialis*, has reddish eyes and distinct colour change from chest to abdomen. Robust Frog, *S. robusta*, has high-pitched call of paired chirps.

**HABITAT**
UNDER LOGS
& LEAF LITTER

**FOOD**
INSECTS

# Australian Bullfrog

*Rana daemeli* (= Damel's frog)

**Length:** ♀ 5.8–8.1; ♂ 4.3–5.8 cm

**Identification:** Large, long frog with narrow, triangular head. Back is smooth and bronze-coloured, with a skin fold from behind the eye to the back of the hindleg. There is a dark stripe from the nostril past the large tympanum, and a pale stripe along the upper lip. The underside is white, speckled brown. The digits have small discs, the fingers are unwebbed and the toes fully webbed.

**Call:** Repeated *yap…yap* or *quack…quack*.

**Where found:** Cape York Peninsula of northern Qld, and eastern Arnhem Land, NT.

**Habits:** Lives amongst waterside vegetation, jumps into water when disturbed and is a powerful swimmer. Lays several thousand eggs, which float on surface. The gold and black tadpole grows to 6.0 cm.

**Notes:** Australia's only representative of a group common in other parts of the world. Calling male's vocal sac lies on both sides of throat.

**Status:** Secure.

**Similar species:** The Striped Rocket-frog, *L. nasuta*, is similar in shape, but its main skin fold does not run uninterrupted from the eye.

IAN MORRIS

**HABITAT**
WATERSIDE
VEGETATION

**FOOD**
INSECTS &
SMALL LIFE

174

# Cane Toad

*Bufo marinus* (= marine toad)

**Length:** ♀ 9.0–25.0; ♂ 7.5–11.0 cm

**Identification:** Large to enormous toad, with a large, short, rounded head. Skin of the back very warty and dry, coloured pale brown, and covered with darker blotches. Large, swollen gland forms a lump behind each side of head. Underside is creamy and grainy, with dark blotches. The eyelid is warty, the pupil is horizontal and the iris golden. The fingers are stubby and lack webbing, the toes are webbed at their bases.

**Call:** Purring; *pop-pop-pop.*

**Where found:** Various habitats<sup>G</sup>, from Coffs Harbour, NSW, across northeastern Qld to Borroloola, NT.

**Habits:** Active at night. Will eat food that does not move. Indifferent to human presence. Glands behind head produce toxin<sup>G</sup> which poisons most animals attempting to eat it. A female may lay 35 000 eggs in a season, in long chains in water. Tadpoles are all-black.

**Notes:** Released in Qld in 1935 to help control cane beetle. Can live and reproduce in a variety of habitats.

**Status:** Expanding its range.

**Similar species:** Dry, warty skin, large glands behind head and horizontal pupils distinguish Cane Toad from burrowing frogs.

**HABITAT** TOWN & COUNTRY

**FOOD** INSECTS & SMALL LIFE

# Fish

An animal is a fish if it:

- has a backbone and a skull
- absorbs oxygen through gills
- is cold-blooded
- has fins
- has tough skin with scales
- has an internal flotation device

## Where and when

Australia's 47 000 km coastline and its tropical and temperate seas create a diversity of habitats for fish. A fish may live in one habitat or move from place to place in search of food and mates. Estuaries and protected bays are breeding and nursery grounds for many species that live elsewhere as adults. Like all animals, fish are most active when feeding. For carnivores, this depends on the tides and the habits of their prey.

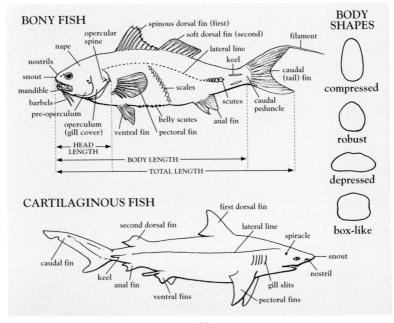

# Marine fish groups

Fish can be divided into two main groups.

*Cartilaginous* fish have skeletons made of gristle and five or more pairs of gill slits. Their skin is covered with tooth-like scales called denticles. An oil-filled liver helps with flotation. Most bear live young.
Chondrichthyes  11 orders including:

| | |
|---|---|
| Orectolobiformes | carpet sharks, wobbegongs |
| Carchariniformes | whaler sharks, hammerheads |
| Lamniformes | Whale Sharks, white pointers |
| Torpediniformes | Numb Rays, electric rays |
| Myliobatiformes | stingrays, Manta Ray |
| Rhinobatiformes | shovelnose rays, fiddler rays |

*Bony fish* have skeletons made of bone and one pair of gill openings. Their skin is covered with overlapping scales. Gas-filled swim bladders control flotation. Most lay eggs.
Osteichthyes  20 orders including:

| | |
|---|---|
| Anguilliformes | eels |
| Siluriformes | catfish |
| Aulopiformes | Sergeant Baker |
| Batrachoidiformes | frogfish |
| Bercyformes | roughies, pineapplefish |
| Syngnathiformes | seahorses, flutemouths |
| Scorpaeniformes | scorpionfish, lionfish |
| Perciformes | perch-like fish (150 families) |
| Pleuronectidae | soles, flounders |
| Tetraodontiformes | pufferfish, leatherjackets |

# Whale Shark

*Rhincodon typus*

GEOFF TAYLOR

**Length:** To 15+ m

**Weight:** 15+ tonnes

**Identification:** Broad head about ¼ of total length; snout rounded; eyes very small; 5 long, wide gill slits. Shark is blue-grey to brownish with white to yellowish spots and pale stripes.

**Where found:** Cruising tropical and cooler oceans; Ningaloo Marine Park, WA.

**Habits:** Feeds on macro-plankton[G], small fish and squid which are gulped in and strained out by sieve tissue in the gill structures. Eggs are in cases 30+ cm long.

**Notes:** The largest living fish; seen at Pt Hicks, Vic., and the NSW south coast but most commonly at Ningaloo. Closely related to carpetsharks having ridges along its back similar to some of these. Harmless; docile. Usually seen alone.

**Status:** Vulnerable[G].

**HABITAT**
OPEN SEA

**FOOD**
SQUID &
SMALL FISH

# Grey Nurse Shark

*Carcharias taurus*

**Length:** To 3.6 m

**Identification:** Large, rather stout body. Eyes small. Conical snout, teeth long and awl-like. Anal fin and 2 dorsals similar size. Large caudal fin, top part much longer. Back, grey to grey-brown; underbelly is dirty white. Juveniles may have reddish spots on rear half of body and tail fin.

**Where found:** Subtropical to cool temperate waters, from the surf zone to 190 m.

**Habits:** Mainly night active; feeds in inshore⁶ gutters. Gives birth to 2 live young, 100 cm long, 1 from each uterus. Young develop from eggs within the mother, the 2 most advanced embryos eat other developing young and unfertilised eggs.

**Notes:** Slow, strong swimmer. Probably not dangerous.

**Status:** Endangered and protected in Australian seas.

**HABITAT**
CONTINENTAL
SHELF – SEA

**FOOD**
FISH

# Port Jackson Shark

*Heterodontus portusjacksoni*

**Length:** To 1.6 m

**Identification:** Tapering body with box-like head; ridges above the eye; mouth small with sharp grasping and rear grinding teeth. Two dorsal fins, each with strong spine. Large pectoral fins. Grey to light brown body with dark marks on snout and below eye.

**Where found:** Southern waters to 240 m. Common in shallow rocky, sandy, muddy and seagrass areas.

**Habits:** Carnivore<sup>G</sup>, eating sea urchins, molluscs<sup>G</sup>, crustaceans<sup>G</sup>, and fish. Breeds in shallow waters during winter; mating generally occurs at night; 18 eggs have hard, brown case bound in double spiral ridge. Eggs are wedged into rocks.

**Notes:** Empty egg-cases are frequently found on tide lines. Dorsal fin spines are slightly venomous<sup>G</sup>.

**Status:** Common.

**HABITAT**
ROCKY
AREAS

**FOOD**
MOLLUSCS
& FISH

# Wobbegong Shark

*Orectolobus ornatus*

**Length:** 1o 3 m

**Identification:** Highly camouflaged fish with flattened head; sensitive fringe of 2–4 fleshy lobes above upper lip both sides; long simple nasal barbels[G]. Broad, almost terminal[G] mouth. 2 dorsal fins, almost equal in size; 5 gill slits.

## Where found:
Bottom dwelling sharks; mainly inshore shallow tropical and cooler waters among reefs and weedbeds.

## Habits:
Sluggish, rests during the day, feeding at night on small rock fish and crabs. Harmless unless provoked. Bears live young.

**Notes:** The tough skin is patterned with warm browns and greys. Known as carpetsharks. Anglers report that the animal gives a grunting noise as it tries to throw the hook.

**Status:** Common.

**HABITAT**
ROCK & CORAL REEFS

**FOOD**
ROCK FISH & CRABS

181

# Manta Ray

*Manta birostris* (= two-beaked cloak)

**Width:** To 6.5 m

**Weight:** To 2 t

**Identification:** Dark blue-black above; white below. Two fins extend in front of head. Pectoral fins form long, pointed wings. Short, slender tail with no spines.

**Where found:** Offshore tropical waters, sometimes near reefs.

**Habits:** Surface dwelling, open sea fish. Moves gracefully. Makes spectacular leaps from the water with a thunderous splash on re-entry. Head fins sweep water and plankton into its huge mouth. Females bear live young.

**Notes:** Largest ray in the world.

**Status:** Secure.

**HABITAT**
OPEN SEA

**FOOD**
PLANKTON

# Masked Stingaree

*Urolophus sp.*

**Width:** 40+ cm

**Identification:** Sandy to muddy brown, pale under-surface with pale brown edge; this shade forms the mask. Disc usually flattened and rounded. Strong, toothed dorsal spine with venomous tissue set ahead of the tail. Teeth flat and broad, used for crushing shelled molluscs.

**Where found:** On sandy and muddy sand flats of beaches, estuaries and lagoons, at depths of 1–30 m.

**Habits:** Very timid, lies partially covered by sand, gravel, mud on the bottom. Active by day and night. When approached it dashes away in a cloud of sand, but will attack if provoked. Gives birth to live young.

**Notes:** The toothed spine may cause severe cuts and bleeding. The slash causes the venomous tissue to tear away and it is left in the wound. This is thought to have evolved a hundred or more million years ago as a protection against bottom-feeding sharks and marine reptiles. A tourniquet may be required. Irrigate with hot salt water and clean the wound thoroughly; seek medical attention.

**Status:** Common.

**HABITAT**
SAND &
GRAVEL

**FOOD**
MOLLUSCS &
CRUSTACEANS

# Eastern Fiddler Ray

*Trygonorrhina fasciata* (= banded nosed-stingray)

**Length:** To 1.2 m

**Identification:** Broad, diamond-shaped disc with rounded snout. Two dorsal fins; tail fin has upper lobe. Five pairs of gill slits. Olive green above; blue-grey bands edged with brown. Broad band between eyes and triangular or oval patch on head above eyes.

**Where found:** South-eastern coastal waters; bays, seagrass beds, estuaries.

**Habits:** Feeds on molluscs, crustaceans and other bottom dwelling invertebrates. Will cover itself with sand or silt.

**Status:** Common.

**HABITAT** SEAGRASS & ESTUARIES

**FOOD** CRUSTACEANS & INVERTEBRATES

# Numb Ray

*Hypnos monopterygium* (= one-winged sleep-inducer)

**Length:** 60 cm

**Identification:**
Rounded disc with large pectoral fins joined to head. Grey to brown to black above; yellowish below. Rounded ventral fins at base of short tail. Two dorsal fins and tail fin close together. Five pairs of gill slits. Small eyes.

**Where found:**
From shallow muddy estuaries to offshore depths in temperate waters from SE Qld to WA.

**Habits:** Weak swimmer that lies on bottom, usually buried. Feeds on fish, and small marine animals. Pounces on and wraps body around prey. Stuns or kills prey with electric shocks. Female bears live young.

**Notes:** Has large electric organs on head. Can discharge a series of shocks that become progressively weaker.

**Status:** Common.

**HABITAT**
ESTUARIES
& OPEN SEA

**FOOD**
FISH &
MARINE ANIMALS

# Striped Catfish

*Plotosus anguillaris*

**Where found:** Tropical and subtropical rivers, estuaries and rock and coral reefs. Very active after river level rises due to rains or melting snow.

**Habits:** Feed on small fish, crustaceans and algae; often lie near bottom in almost sold masses, and travel in dense, rolling pods[G] near the surface.

**Length:** 50–90 cm

**Weight:** To 5 kg

**Identification:** Generally gleaming black with body-length creamy stripes. 8 barbels: 2 nasal barbels reach the eyes. Lacks scales. Venomous glands at base of dorsal and pectoral spines.

**Notes:** Handle with care. Spines can inflict very painful wounds. Induce these to bleed freely; may need antihistamine injection. Cormorants feed on young eeltailed catfish.

**Status:** Abundant.

**HABITAT** RIVERS & REEFS

**FOOD** SMALL FISH & CRUSTACEANS

# Green Moray Eel

*Gymnothorax prasinus*

**Length:** To 1.5 m

**Weight:** 8 kg

**Identification:**
Powerful, elongate[G] body, somewhat compressed; small gill slits. A small head on a greatly swollen neck; eyes very small; mouth large; teeth strong, long and sharp. Body, dorsal and caudal fins covered with brown to greenish skin.

**Where found:**
Two populations (see map); rocky, weedy subtidal[G] habitats.

**Habits:** Can be fiercely aggressive if disturbed. Carnivores, they prey on smaller animals; effective scavengers[G]. Small prey is swallowed whole, jaws lock onto larger prey. A muscular knot forms at the tail and moves along the body, finally causing flesh to be torn away.

**Notes:** Lateral line is absent but sensory[G] pores on its jaws are outlined by dark pigment. Fluorescent green skin colour may change according to depth of water and fades to dark tan on death.

**Status:** Common.

**HABITAT**
ROCKY
REEFS

**FOOD**
FISH &
CRUSTACEANS

# Sergeant Baker

*Aulopus purpurissatus*

**Length:** To 68 cm

**Identification:** Heavy bodied, compressed fish. Speckled crimson, red and orange; sail-like first dorsal fin; males have long ray on first dorsal. Large head with gaping mouth; teeth sharp, fine and curved. Lateral line well defined; eyes, orange/crimson.

**Where found:** Rocky and coral bottoms from shallow inlets to 250 m deep.

**Habits:** Carnivorous; diet includes molluscs, crustaceans and other smaller fish.

**Notes:** The head is about $1/3$ body length. Sexes are different in colour. Rear margin of scales is spiny.

**Status:** Common.

**HABITAT**
REEF &
RUBBLE

**FOOD**
MOLLUSCS &
SMALL FISH

# Eastern Frogfish

*Batrachomoeus sp.*

**Length:**
To 30 cm

**Identification:**
Stout fish compressed towards tail. Scales absent; skin covered with thick mucus; skin loose with fleshy fringes, flaps and tentacles; skin blotches arranged in several broad bands. Head

broad, short snout with eyes on top; spines on each gill cover; mouth small.

**Where found:** Inshore rocky reefs, coral reef flats and weedy areas. Often caught near wharf pilings. From subtidal habitat to 150 m deep.

**Habits:** Solitary, well camouflaged fish feeding on small fish, crustaceans and echinoderms[G].

**Notes:** Bears a superficial resemblance to the Stonefish. Not venomous, but spines on gill covers can inflict painful wounds. A feeble swimmer, it depends on ambush to capture prey. It makes a frog-like noise when caught.

**Status:** Unknown, probably common.

**HABITAT**
WEEDY
REEFS

**FOOD**
SMALL FISH &
CRUSTACEANS

# Roughy

*Trachichthys australis*

**Length:** To 18 cm

**Identification:** Reddish to orange-brown with dark bar across the gill covers. Compressed circular profile with large, very rough and bony head; eyes nearly half length of head; large, angled mouth; sharp spines on the gill covers. Scales small and very rough; 9–12 very large scutes[G] under belly. Tail is deeply forked.

**Where found:** Temperate, shallow coastal reefs and rocky bottoms to 30 m deep.

**Habits:** Carnivorous; feeds at night. If disturbed can release a milky substance into the water which disables fish.

**Notes:** Frequently caught on hook and line along the coast from south Qld to Lancelin, WA.

**Status:** Common.

**HABITAT**
ROCKY REEF
& RUBBLE

**FOOD**
FISH & SMALL
CRUSTACEANS

# Pineapplefish

*Cleidopus gloriamaris*

**Length:** To 28 cm

**Identification:** Dark net-like pattern on edges of large, yellow, plate-like, bony scales which have central ridge spines. Head encased in bone; snout round and broad; mouth small with light-producing organ at lower jaw corners; teeth small.

**Where found:** On soft bottom, open estuaries, bays and continental shelf, at depths of 3–150 m.

**Habits:** Greenish light, which attracts small crustaceans at night on which the fish feed, comes from bacteria produced by an organ on each side of the lower lip.

**Notes:** Sometimes called Knightfish or Pineconefish; makes a loud creaking noise when disturbed. Spines on the dorsal fin lean alternately left and right.

**Status:** Believed to be secure.

**HABITAT** ESTUARIES

**FOOD** SMALL CRUSTACEANS

# Big-belly Seahorse

*Hippocampus abdominalis*

**Length:** To 30 cm

**Identification:** Body wrapped in a series of bony plates. Tail prehensile[G], gripping seagrasses and other parts of habitat. Head angled downwards; snout like a tube, about half of head length. Single central dorsal fin. Colour ranges from purple to brown, orange or yellow; tail banded, sides black splotched.

**Where found:** Shallow inlets and rocky areas with weed over mud and sand areas; at depths of 5–30 m.

**Habits:** Seahorses swim slowly in upright position propelled by dorsal and pectoral fins. Feed on planktonic crustaceans and larval[G] fish.

**Notes:** Male broods the eggs in an enclosed pouch on the underside of the belly and gives birth to live young.

**Status:** Common.

**HABITAT**
WEEDY
AREAS

**FOOD**
PLANKTON &
MARINE LARVAE

# Common Sea Dragon

*Phyllopteryx taeniolatus*

**Length:** 46+ cm

**Identification:**
Body shaped like wavy line; thick trunk; usually reddish with yellow spots and bluish bars on sides of the trunk. Dorsal fin near to tail; flattened spines and flaps resemble fronds of algae[G]. Tail prehensile. Head at slight angle to body; long slender snout. Body covered in bony plates.

**Where found:**
From central NSW to Tas. and Rottnest Is., WA, in beds of algae along rocky reefs to 50 m deep.

**Habits:** Eggs on under-surface of the tail, held by layer of skin, are brooded by the male. Feeds on small and planktonic crustaceans.

**Notes:** Has variable colouring and changes form during growth. Travel is by rippling movements of dorsal and pectoral fins. Also called Weedy Sea dragon.

**Status:** Common.

**HABITAT**
WEEDY BEDS
AMONG REEFS

**FOOD**
PLANKTON &
MARINE LARVAE

# Scorpion Cod

*Scorpaena papillosa*

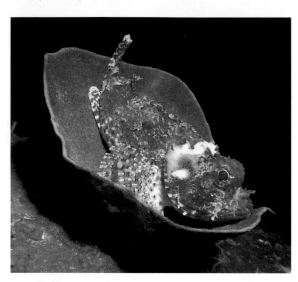

Fleshy flaps of skin on nostril, above the eye and on some lateral line scales. Strong dorsal fin spines; leading spines venomous.

**Where found:** To 130 m deep, over stony bottoms.

**Habits:** Solitary or in small groups feeding along the bottom and around rocky reefs for crustaceans and small fish.

**Length:** 36+ cm

**Identification:** Robust, tapering, reddish to reddish-brown body; upper body colour blotched; pale underside. Head, moderate sized; jaw half of head length; teeth tiny in upper and lower bands. 5 spines on cheek; 2 dorsal spines on each gill cover; 5 spines below each eye.

**Notes:** The Scorpion Cod (or Red or Southern) Rock-cod is a member of a large family–at least 15 groups with similar characteristics in Australian waters.

**Status:** Common.

**HABITAT**
WEEDY
REEFS

**FOOD**
SMALL FISH &
CRUSTACEANS

# Stonefish

*Synanceia horrida*

**Length:** To 33 cm

**Identification:**
Brown/grey mud-like robust fish; skin, warty, almost shapeless. Older fish have algae and hydroids (small marine animals called sea firs) growing on them. Very large paddle-like pectoral fins; sharp venomous dorsal spines. High placed small eyes; large mouth.

**Where found:** Bays, estuaries and reef flats, on mud, sand or among rocks or coral, at depths of 1–40 m.

**Habits:** Well camouflaged, uses pectoral fins to bury itself leaving only eyes and dorsal area clear. Ambushes crustacean or fish prey.

**Notes:** Dorsal spine venom is of tiny grains. Pressure on the spine forces out a holding plug of tissue, releasing and injecting a surge of venom. Victim's blood pressure falls, breathing is irregular, followed by partial paralysis and sometimes death. First aid is to penetrate wound with an acid which will break down the venom. Urgent medical treatment required. An antidote is available.

**Status:** Common.

**HABITAT**
ROCK &
CORAL REEFS

**FOOD**
FISH &
CRUSTACEANS

# Lionfish

*Pterois volitans*

**Length:** To 38 cm

**Identification:** Behind long, feathery dorsal and pectoral fins is a robust, compressed body, patterned with brown to reddish-brown bands. Head large; mouth gaping; pattern, mask-like. Dorsal spines venomous.

**Where found:** Various habitats from tropical and subtropical reef and coral waters, to estuaries and bays, such as Moreton Bay, Qld, at depths of 8–40 m.

**Habits:** Moves slowly using its pectoral fins to guide prey to within range of its mouth. Rapidly, jaws open, gill covers are flung open, floor of mouth drops and the surge of water drags prey in.

**Notes:** Lives in grottoes and under large branches of coral. Venom causes severe pain. Has several other common names, including Devilfish, Firefish and Butterfly Cod.

**Status:** Common.

**HABITAT**
CORAL
REEFS

**FOOD**
FISH, SQUID &
CRUSTACEANS

# Butterfly Gurnard

*Lepidotrigla vanessa*

**Length:** To 28 cm

**Identification:** Tapered body has a reddish pattern on a buff ground. Head is small with box-like cross-section; encased in bone; snout concave<sup>G</sup>; mouth small. Pectoral fins open like large fans edged with fluorescent blue; dorsal fin in two highly patterned parts, with large, dark, pale-edged blotch. Scales small; lateral line scales have spines.

**Where found:** Bottom dwelling fish at 20–100 m deep from Newcastle, NSW, to southwestern Australia.

**Habits:** Feeds on bottom-dwelling crustaceans and worms. Armoured snout adapted to act as shovel.

**Notes:** Largest member of a group having similar characteristics. Most often taken in trawls in Bass Strait.

**Status:** Common.

**HABITAT**
GRAVEL
BOTTOM

**FOOD**
WORMS &
CRUSTACEANS

 # Sand Flathead

*Neoplatycephalus bassensis*

**Length:** To 46 cm

**Weight:** 3.1 kg

**Identification:** Long, depressed body, sandy brown above, pale below; covered with mucus. Flattened head about ⅓ of body length; eye with small flap; large mouth with small, pointed teeth. Gill covers have 2 long cutting spines, lower twice as long as upper. Small scales from eyes to tail; lateral line scales larger. Two dorsal fins with sharp spines.

**Where found:** From Newcastle, NSW, to eastern SA in sandy bays, estuaries and coastal waters to 100 m.

**Habits:** Well camouflaged on sandy bottoms; ambushes small sandflat fish while partially buried in the sand. Will also pursue prey.

**Notes:** Sand Flathead's colour and habit of burying itself in the sand, fully or partly, camouflage it from predators[G] and prey.

**Status:** Common.

**HABITAT** SAND & GRAVEL

**FOOD** FISH & CRUSTACEANS

# Red Emperor

*Lutjanus sebae*

**Length:** 1.1 m
**Weight:** 20+ kg

**Identification:** Deep, compressed, perch-like body. The clear markings of the juvenile (photo), become overtaken by an overall deepening redness with age. Sharply pointed dorsal

and anal fins become rounded with age; reddish fins are fringed in white. Scales start behind the eyes. Mouth is moderately large with canine[G] teeth in front row, upper jaw.

**Where found:** From Moreton Bay, Qld, north in tropical waters. Habitat, deep waters (15–100 m) of reef edges, gravel bottoms.

**Habits:** Form schools of similar-sized fish. Some reefs have only large fish while others have small fish.

**Notes:** Feed whenever opportunity arises, on fish, squid, crustaceans and invertebrates[G].

**Status:** Accessible reefs become overfished, but species still common.

**HABITAT**
CORAL
REEFS

**FOOD**
FISH, SQUID &
CRUSTACEANS

 # Barramundi

*Lates calcarifer*

**Length:** 1.6 m

**Weight:** To 50 kg

**Identification:** Stretched elliptical shape; ranges between metallic deep grey-green to silver according to habitat. Marked concave slope from head to humped back. Large mouth; bands of small teeth; eyes high on head glow orange-red. Two dorsal fins, first with strong spines; very sharp serrated gill covers.

**Where found:** North around tropical coast from Maryborough, Qld; in freshwater billabongs, lagoons, and rivers and down estuaries into the sea.

**Habits:** Eggs are laid in estuarine swamps; hatch in less than a day, move upstream at age 1 year to grow to 3 years old, then move to the ocean. Males become female at 5–7 years then enter mangrove swamps to lay eggs. Prey on crustaceans and smaller fish, particularly mullet.

**Notes:** Life history shows how a species depends for survival on a chain of different habitats: rivers, mangroves, estuaries and ocean.

**Status:** Common, but some habitat is threatened.

**HABITAT**
LAGOONS &
ESTUARIES

**FOOD**
SMALL AQUATIC
ANIMALS

# Blackspot Goatfish

*Parupeneus porphyreus*

**Length:** to 50 cm

**Identification:** Elongate fish with arched back and paired sensory barbels. Base colour white with 4 reddish-green stripes from nose to second dorsal fin; black spot across hind dorsal area, often with yellow blotch in front. Colour varies with mood or day/night. Two dorsal fins; caudal fin forked.

**Where found:** Inshore reef waters foraging across reef flats to a depth of 20 m.

**Habits:** Form foraging schools; when isolated, an individual will school with other species. Food is small invertebrates such as crustaceans and worms.

**Notes:** Named for the pair of barbels which droop from the chin like a goat's beard.

**Status:** Common.

**HABITAT**
REEF
WATERS

**FOOD**
WORMS &
CRUSTACEANS

# Moses Perch

*Lutjanus russelli*

**Length:** To 50 cm

**Weight:** To 10 kg

**Identification:** Oblong, compressed fish, pinkish in ocean, olive in estuaries. Black patch below rear third of dorsal fin across the lateral line; yellow pectoral, anal and ventral fins. Upper jaw with canine[G] teeth; gill cover very sharp.

**Where found:** In subtropical and tropical estuaries, bays and reefs with 5–35 m water.

**Habits:** An active hunter in estuaries where Barramundi and Mangrove Jack share the habitat. Preys on smaller fish, crustaceans and squid. Schools in large numbers about inshore reefs but also in pairs. Found under ledges during daylight.

**Notes:** Name comes from a piece of biblical history in relation to the black patch. It was, however, St Peter and not Moses whose fingers were supposed to burn spots into the fish Tilapia in the Sea of Galilee.

**Status:** Common.

**HABITAT**
TROPICAL
REEFS

**FOOD**
FISH, SQUID &
CRUSTACEANS

# Painted Sweetlip

*Diagramma pictum* or *Diagramma labiosa*

**Length:** To 80 cm

**Weight:** To 4.5 kg

**Identification:** Grey-blue, oblong, compressed fish; thick lips; bands of pointed teeth; most of head is scale-covered; profile of head convex⁶. Single dorsal fin with strong spines; second spine more than twice as long as the first. Sometimes bronze colour; speckled with small olive spots.

**Where found:** In dense schools over sand beds of coral patch reefs.

**Habits:** Dense schools browse at night on invertebrates, and take crustaceans and small fish.

**Notes:** It has been reported that dark blotches on the skin change colour according to the fish's mood. Colours change markedly during growth. Young fish are yellow-brown with horizontal sooty-brown bands.

**Status:** Common.

| HABITAT | CORAL REEFS |
| --- | --- |

| FOOD | CRUSTACEANS & SMALL FISH |
| --- | --- |

*Choerodon fasciatus*

**Length:** 30 cm

**Identification:** Deep-bodied, compressed fish with steeply rising head; small mouth with strong, tusk-like canines. Body colour purple-blue into greenish grey; 6–9 red to orange vertical bars; tail scarlet grading from a yellow-green patch. Dorsal, ventral and tail fins scarlet, edged with blue. A heavy layer of mucus covers the scales.

**Where found:** Shelters under coral growths; at high tide, ranges out to reef flats and into channels at depths of 5–30 m.

**Habits:** Forages among living coral and coral rubble for invertebrate food: molluscs, crustaceans, worms, sea urchins. Highly territorial.

**Notes:** Can become a nuisance to divers as it follows them to take invertebrates stirred up by the diver's movements.

**Status:** Common (valued aquarium species).

 **HABITAT**
CORAL
REEF FLATS

 **FOOD**
LIVING CORAL
& INVERTEBRATES

# Blue-barred Parrotfish

*Scarus ghobban*

**Length:** 1 m

**Weight:** 5 kg

**Identification:** Elongate-oval compressed fish with underlying body colour of orange-tan; blue centres of scales form vertical bars; head mostly orange-pink with blue wavy lines around mouth and through the eyes. Teeth in each jaw are almost fused[G] to form a beak, like a parrot's. Large scales are mucus-covered.

**Where found:** Shelters beneath and feeds on coral outcrops and at high tide across reef flats. Occurs throughout southwestern Pacific coral areas at depths of 1–30 m.

**Habits:** Highly territorial.

Bites chunks out of living coral and breaks this down to fine sand extracting organic matter, such as algae, before excreting sand. It also works through coral rubble which may contain organisms.

**Notes:** Responsible with other parrotfish and wrasses for much of the coral sand found in reef areas. Fish colour is very variable.

**Status:** Common.

**HABITAT** CORAL REEFS

**FOOD** LIVING CORAL & ORGANISMS

205

# Bannerfish

*Heniochus acuminatus*

**Length:** 25 cm

**Identification:** Very deep compressed body with trailing filament from fourth spine of dorsal fin. Body shining white with 2 broad purple-black bands accenting form and size of central white crescent; bright yellow soft dorsal and tail fins. Profile of head concave; purple-black patch across snout and another linking and crossing the eyes.

**Where found:** In and about caverns from Moreton Bay, Qld, north.

**Habits:** Stays near to protective coral reef and grottoes. Feeds on invertebrates and algae growing about coral, as well as browsing the corals. It is a slow mover.

**Notes:** Fine example of disruptive[G] coloration.

**Status:** Common (valued aquarium species).

**HABITAT**
CORAL
REEFS

**FOOD**
ALGAE &
INVERTEBRATES

# Emperor Angelfish

*Pomacanthus imperator*

**Length:** 38 cm

**Identification:** Brilliantly coloured, oblong, compressed fish. Snout shaped to forage amongst coral; teeth fine and slender. Gill cover with strong spine. Tail fin rounded.

**Where found:** Subtropical and tropical Australian coast, Kalbarri, WA, to Iluka, NSW, around coral and rocky reefs.

**Habits:** These fish are territorial[G] and centre on caverns and grottoes near surge and tidal channels and gutters. They feed on sponges, sea tulips, and organisms and algae that grow on coral.

**Notes:** Adult patterning is very different from the juvenile patterns. These are dark blue with white markings.

**Status:** Moderately common.

**HABITAT**
CORAL
REEFS

**FOOD**
ALGAE &
SPONGES

# Brown Anemonefish

*Amphiprion akindynos*

**Length:** 12 cm

**Identification:** Light to dark chocolate-brown body with 2 black-edged white or pale blue bars; creamy-yellow under head and belly; juveniles have 3 bars. Slightly hollowed tail fin.

**Where found:** In and about stinging tentacles of anemones growing on coral reefs from the Capricorn Group of the Great Barrier Reef to Torres Strait, at depths of 1–20 m.

**Habits:** Chemicals in mucus coating fish's body prevent anemones from stinging. Fish rely on stinging anemones for protection, and protect anemones from other feeding fish. Pairs or small groups feed on planktonic crustaceans and algae growing on coral. Eggs are laid on stone beneath the tentacles.

**Notes:** All are born male and change with age to female. In typical group, large female mates with smaller male. When female dies, male changes sex and next dominant male becomes partner.

**Status:** Common.

**HABITAT**
CORAL
REEFS

**FOOD**
PLANKTONIC
CRUSTACEANS

208

# Zebrafish

*Enoplosus armatus*

**Length:** 25 cm

**Identification:**
Deep, compressed body. Mouth, small in upturned snout; profile of head concave; slender teeth in both jaws. 2 tall dorsal fins, first with venomous spines; leading edges of fins often pinkish. Scales are very small; lateral line very clear. Strongly marked with about 8 vertical black bars on a silvery-white body.

**Where found:** Coastal rocky reefs in warm and cool temperate waters, from inshore to 100 m, and around jetties and wharves.

**Habits:** Live as individuals or in schools. A carnivore preferring crustaceans and worms.

**Notes:** Sometimes misnamed John Dory. Handle this fish with care. A wound from venomous spines gives a sharp prickling sensation followed by aching and swelling.

**Status:** Common and abundant on inshore rocky and seagrass beds.

**HABITAT**
ROCKY
REEFS

**FOOD**
WORMS &
CRUSTACEANS

# Eastern Stargazer

*Kathetostoma laeve*

**Length:** To 75 cm

**Weight:** 8 kg

**Identification:** Large head with upturned face; small eyes set in top of head. Mouth large and vertical; lips with narrow fleshy fringe; row of prominent canine teeth in lower jaw; upper teeth, fine outer row, inner row of canines. Blotched greyish-tan, tapering body, white below. Scales absent. Single, long dorsal fin without spines; pectoral fins large. Fins have white margins.

**Where found:** Occurs from shallow, sandy beds at 1m to depth of 60 m; in seagrass beds of estuaries, lagoons and bays.

**Habits:** Using pectoral fins, buries itself in sand with eyes and jaws clear. A poor swimmer, uses ambush to take prey, such as crustaceans and large fish.

**Notes:** Location of eyes gives its name of the 'Stargazer'. Aggressive, has been known to bite divers.

**Status:** Probably common.

**HABITAT** SEAGRASS BEDS

**FOOD** LARGE FISH & CRUSTACEANS

# Crested Morwong

*Cheilodactylus vestitus*

**Length:** 30 cm

**Identification:** Small head with two bony 'horns' in adults, one above lip and one in front of eyes; head rises steeply to a crowning dorsal fin; straight taper to tail. Mouth small with thick, yellow fleshy lips ringed with brown; small pointed teeth. Body, white with 4 black bands. Fourth spine of dorsal fin very long; tail fin forked.

**Where found:** Among jetties and wharves, estuaries, inshore and offshore reefs to 20 m deep.

**Habits:** Reef and bottom feeders on molluscs and worms.

**Notes:** Mainly found on its own, but sometimes in pairs or small groups.

**Status:** Common.

**HABITAT**
ROCK &
CORAL REEFS

**FOOD**
MOLLUSCS
& WORMS

# White Trevally

*Pseudocaranx dentex*

**Length:** 94 cm

**Weight:** 10 kg

**Identification:** Elliptical, strongly compressed, shimmering bluish-silver body covered with very small scales; scales towards end of very clear lateral line enlarge to become sharp scutes. Head moderate size; mouth smallish and nearly horizontal; teeth small. Dorsal fin in two parts; second dorsal and anal fins very similar. Tail deeply forked. Black blotch high on gill cover.

**Where found:** Ocean fish found in schools south from central coasts in warm temperate water, at depths of 80–200 m.

**Habits:** Young collect in coastal inlets where they are frequently netted by estuary anglers. Adult is an aggressive predator.

**Notes:** Streamlined, fast swimmers.

**Status:** Common.

**HABITAT**
OPEN REEF
WATER

**FOOD**
FISH &
PRAWNS

# Peacock Sole

*Pardachirus pavoninus* (=peacock-spotted fish)

**Length:** To 22 cm

**Identification:** A flattened fish with both eyes on right side of body. Left side of body lies underneath. Snout extends over mouth, which is twisted into a slanted, sideways position. Fins extend from behind head along edges of body. Upper side of body is pale brown with indistinct darker blotches underlying small fawn-coloured spots, some with dark centres.

**Where found:** Coastal sand or mudflats in northern tropical seas.

**Habits:** Feeds on small fish and invertebrates. Usually lies buried with only eyes showing. Milky fluid from toxin glands along fin bases can stun predators. Sometimes found in groups.

**Notes:** Newly hatched soles swim upright and have an eye on either side of the head. The eyes gradually move to one side of the body as the fish grows.

**Status:** Common.

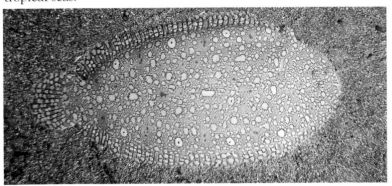

**HABITAT**
SAND &
MUDFLATS

**FOOD**
FISH &
INVERTEBRATES

 # Porcupine Fish

*Dicotylichthys myersi*

**Length:**
To 45 cm

**Identification:**
Inflatable, globe-shaped body splotched with brown and darker spots; white underbody. At night, turns uniform greyish cream with slightly darker back. Spines

that can be erected cover body except for face. Jaws powerful; teeth fused and chisel-like. Fins transparent yellow. Swims using small single dorsal and anal fins.

**Where found:** Tropical waters, coral and rocky reefs.

**Habits:** Feeds from dusk until dawn, singly or in loose groups. Swims slowly, body angled down browsing on rocks and cliff edges as well as sea floor searching for molluscs, crustaceans and sea urchins. Spends daylight sheltering beneath overhangs. It can inflate itself to 3 times its normal size with water or air, causing its spines to become erect.

**Notes:** Little is known of its life history. This fish is poisonous: DO NOT EAT.

**Status:** Common.

 **HABITAT**
REEFS &
MUDFLATS

**FOOD**
MOLLUSCS &
CRUSTACEANS

# Rainbow Leatherjacket

*Meuschenia skottowei*

**Length:** 46 cm

**Identification:** Elliptical compressed body with a base coloration of olive-green; vivid blue lines radiate from eyes to snout; a close network of blue lines covers much of the body. Tail and fin edges, 'electric' blue. A yellow patch often lies across the sides. Smaller fish have paler colours. Gill slit small. Mouth small; teeth flat scrapers. Three small spines on each side from the base of the tail. Retractable dorsal spine stands above the eye.

**Where found:** Estuaries, inshore reefs and weed beds of the NSW and south Qld coast.

**Habits:** A solitary fish with little known life history. Feeds on small invertebrates. Teeth are suitable for cutting, scraping and nibbling sponges from a variety of places including from sea tulips.

**Notes:** Colours are highly variable. Also called Six-spined Leatherjacket.

**Status:** Unknown.

**HABITAT**
WEED BEDS
& REEFS

**FOOD**
SPONGES &
INVERTEBRATES

# Land Invertebrates

Over 90% of all animals are invertebrates. These animals without backbones mainly go unnoticed, yet can be found in every Australian habitat. The greatest number of land invertebrates, including insects and spiders, belong to the group Arthropoda.

Ulysses Butterfly

Green Ants

An arthropod has a hard, external skeleton to protect its body. This exoskeleton is shed and replaced each time an arthropod grows larger. Arthropods also have jointed limbs or appendages that are adapted for feeding, moving, holding things and sensing the environment.

St Andrews Cross Spider

Orchard Swallowtail Caterpillar

# scorpions

Class Arachnida

**Length:** may grow to 12+ cm.

**Identification:** Medium to large arthropods that, like spiders, have bodies divided into cephalothorax⁶ and abdomen, but have no waist. The abdomen has a long tail, ending in a sting that is held over the body. The head bears antennae, 6–12 eyes, chelicerae⁶ and a large pair of pedipalps⁶, the final two segments of each forming a grasping pair of pincers.

**Where found:** On ground, in burrows, under rocks and logs, under bark.

**Habits:** Feed on live prey such as insects, spiders, millipedes. Male and female perform mating dance in which male guides female's reproductive opening over a packet of sperm he has deposited on the ground. Female gives birth to live young, which she carries on her back for some weeks.

**Notes:** At night, ultraviolet light highlights scorpions. Australian spp. may cause pain and swelling if they bite humans.

**Similar creatures:** Freshwater crays have pincers, but lack turned-back tail with sting.

JIRI LOCHMAN

**HABITAT**
ANYWHERE
ON GROUND

**FOOD**
SMALL
CREATURES

# millipedes

Class *Diplopoda*

JIRI LOCHMAN

**Length:** up to 10 cm

**Identification:** Small to large arthropods which have two pairs of small legs on each body segment (actually two segments fused together).

**Where found:** Under rocks, logs, bark, leaf litter.

**Habits:** Young stages may have only single pairs of legs on each segment. Many segments can produce a nasty-tasting liquid as a defence against predators. Other defence is to curl up (see photo right). Millipedes usually eat plant material. To mate, male wraps himself around female and passes packet of sperm with special mating legs on his seventh segment into the female's reproductive opening.

**Notes:** Nine groups of millipedes are recorded from Aust. The introduced Black Portuguese Millipede may be a pest in southeastern Aust., eating garden plants and invading houses.

**Similar creatures:** Centipedes have one pair of large legs to each body segment.

JIRI LOCHMAN

**HABITAT**
UNDER LOGS,
LEAVES

**FOOD**
PLANT
MATERIAL

# centipedes

Class *Chilopoda*

**Length:** 1–15 cm

**Identification:** Small to very large arthropods, with from 15 to (occasionally) over 100 pairs of legs on the same number of body segments, according to species. Head bears a pair of antennae, chewing mouthparts. First pair of legs, under first segment, bears poison claws. Final segment bears long, often brightly coloured legs.

**Where found:** Under rocks, bark, in soil or leaf litter.

**Habits:** Prey such as insects, spiders, small frogs and geckos,

PETER MARSACK

is killed by venom from the claws, torn up by the jaws. The male lays a packet of sperm onto a mat he has spun, or places the sperm onto the female's reproductive opening. She guards her eggs until they hatch.

**Notes:** A bite may cause pain, swelling. The house centipede (photo left) is about 5 cm long, has 15 pairs of long legs.

**Similar creatures:** Millipedes appear to have two pairs of legs on each body segment, are non-venomous plant-eaters.

JIRI LOCHMAN

**HABITAT**
ANYWHERE
ON GROUND

**FOOD**
SMALL
CREATURES

# Insects

An animal is an insect if it:

- ✹ has 3 body divisions – head, thorax and abdomen
- ✹ has 3 pairs of walking legs
- ✹ has simple or compound eyes
- ✹ has 1 pair of antennae
- ✹ has 3 pairs of mouth parts forming jaws
- ✹ lays eggs

Most insects have wings and change shape during their life cycle.

## Life cycles

These bugs (below left) will go through gradual changes such as growing larger wings. Other insects go through abrupt changes such as the Cairns Birdwing Butterfly which will change from larva (middle) to a pupa, from which will emerge an adult (right).

STANLEY BREEDEN

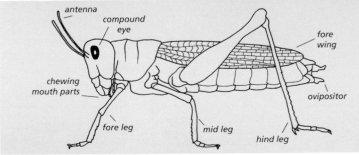

antenna

compound eye

fore wing

chewing mouth parts

ovipositor

fore leg

mid leg

hind leg

# Insect groups

Australian insects can be divided into three main groups based on their life cycle, and whether they have wings.

*Apterygote* insects are wingless and do not change shape as they mature. The young look like adults and use the same habitat and food. Two orders:

| | |
|---|---|
| Archaeognatha | bristletails |
| Thysanura | silverfish |

*Exopterygote* insects have wings that develop on the outside of their bodies. They change gradually through several nymph[G] stages. Fourteen orders including:

| | |
|---|---|
| Odonata | dragonflies, damselflies |
| Blattodea | cockroaches |
| Isoptera | termites |
| Mantodea | mantids |
| Dermaptera | earwigs |
| Orthoptera | grasshoppers, crickets |
| Phasmatodea | stick insects |
| Hemiptera | bugs, cicadas |

*Endopterygote* insects have wings that develop inside their bodies. They undergo several abrupt changes including a grub or caterpillar stage. Ten orders including:

| | |
|---|---|
| Neuroptera | lacewings |
| Coleoptera | beetles |
| Mecoptera | scorpion flies |
| Diptera | flies, mosquitoes |
| Lepidoptera | moths, butterflies |
| Hymenoptera | ants, bees, wasps |

Order *Odonata* (= flies with teeth)

PETER MARSACK

**Length:** 20–150 mm

**Aust. spp.:** 302

**Identification:** Medium to large, slender-bodied, huge-eyed, flying predators[G]. Adults have two pairs of stiff, gauzy wings (held out sideways by resting dragonflies, held along abdomen by damselflies). Head bears tiny antennae, enormous compound eyes, biting and chewing mouthparts. Legs end in claws used to seize prey.

**Where found:** Larvae live in fresh water.

**Life history:** Larvae live in fresh water, have lower lips which shoot out and catch small water animals. Gills, which filter oxygen from water, are hidden in final part of digestive tract in broad-bodied dragonfly larvae, but exposed on tip of abdomen of slender damselfly larvae. After up to 15 moults, larvae crawl up plant stem into air and adults emerge.

**Habits:** Adults active during day, especially near water. Perch or cruise, darting after flying insects. Mating takes place in "wheel" position (see photo). Female lays eggs in water while flying, sometimes joined to male.

**Notes:** Female may be duller in colour than male and wander further from water. Male may defend a territory[G].

**Similar insects:** None.

 **HABITAT** NEAR WATER

 **FOOD** FLYING INSECTS

# cockroaches

Order *Blattodea* (= light-avoiders)

**Length:** 3–70 mm

**Aust. spp.:** 428

**Identification:** Small to large, scuttling and crawling insects with flattened bodies. Native species may have colourful markings. Part of head and thorax shielded by a large plate. Tough forewings overlap and cover gauzy hindwings (some spp. are wingless). Long, spiny legs. Head bears very long antennae, two compound eyes, two simple eyes and chewing mouthparts. One pair of cerci<sup>G</sup> at end of abdomen.

**Where found:** Native spp. under bark, stones, logs, in litter, burrows. Introduced spp. in buildings, sewers.

**Life history:** 12–40 eggs laid in case which may be carried at end of abdomen by female (see photo). Some spp. have live young. Nymphs look like wingless adults and moult several times before developing wing buds.

**Habits:** Introduced spp. eat variety of food at night. Native spp. may feed during day on plant debris.

**Notes:** Native spp. include huge, wingless, burrowing northern Qld cockroach, which feeds its young on dead leaves.

**Similar insects:** Beetles have hard wing covers, which meet down the centre of the back.

**HABITAT**
BUSHLAND,
HOUSES

**FOOD**
PLANTS,
HUMAN FOOD

# termites

Order *Isoptera* (= equal wings)

JIRI LOCHMAN

**Length:** 3–18 mm

**Aust. spp.:** 348

**Identification:** Small to medium-sized, pale, soft-bodied insects. Live in colony<sup>G</sup> of infertile<sup>G</sup>, blind, wingless workers and soldiers, fertile males and females which begin adult life with wings. Head bears beadlike, straight antennae, chewing mouthparts (large in soldiers). There is no waist between the thorax and abdomen.

**Where found:** In timber, underground, or in nests built on ground or in trees.

**Life history:** Nymph hatches from egg, is fed by workers, develops into worker, soldier, or winged male or female which flies from nest. A pair mates, sheds wings and queen lays eggs to begin a new colony.

**Habits:** Termites eat wood, bark, grass and other plant substances. Tiny organisms in their gut tissue digest the tough walls of plant cells.

**Notes:** Colony may consist of over one million insects; queen and king may live for many years. Termites are eaten by many animals, recycle plant material, destroy buildings.

**Similar insects:** Ants have harder, darker bodies with distinct waists. Their antennae have "elbows", and they have compound eyes.

**HABITAT**
TERMITE
NESTS, WOOD

**FOOD**
PLANT
MATERIAL

# mantids

Order *Mantodea* (= like a prophet*)

**Length:** 10–120 mm

**Aust. spp.:** 162

**Identification:** Medium to large, slender, stilt-legged predators, which use spiked forelegs to seize prey. Usually brown or green. Have tough, narrow forewings and gauzy, fanlike hindwings. Some spp. wingless. Head is triangular, moves freely on narrow neck. It bears fine antennae, chewing mouthparts, two very large compound eyes, and three simple eyes.

**Where found:** Usually on leaves, stems or grass, tree trunks or ground.

**Life history:** Female lays eggs into frothy case attached to vegetation or rock. Young mantids (nymphs) are similar to adults, but lack wings.

**Habits:** Waits motionless, then shoots out spiked forearms to grab passing insect.

**Notes:** Many spp. resemble their habitats in colour and pattern. Male may sometimes be eaten by female while mating, but in the wild he usually escapes this fate.

**Similar insects:** Stick insects use forelegs for walking. Some lacewings have grasping forelegs, but have two pairs of membranous wings held roof-like over the body.

* Refers to the praying position of the forelegs when insect is at rest.

STANLEY BREEDEN

 **HABITAT** LEAVES, GRASS

 **FOOD** INSECTS

# grasshoppers and locusts

Order *Orthoptera* (= straight wings)

**Length:** 5–100 mm

**Aust. spp. in order Orthoptera (pp. 14, 15):** 2827

**Identification:** Small to large, leaping insects with large hindlegs. Forewings are tougher, smaller, narrower than gauzy hindwings.

No narrowing between head and thorax. Threadlike antennae, compound eyes, chewing mouthparts. **Grasshoppers** and **locusts** have antennae of less than 30 segments, usually less than half length of body. Females have short ovipositors[G]. There are 1021 spp. in Australia.

**Where found:** On plants, often near ground.

**Life history:** Male calls to attract female. Female digs tip of abdomen into soil, lays groups of 10–200 eggs. Nymph moults 4–6 times before becoming winged adult.

**Habits:** Active during day, feeding on plants.

**Notes:** Calls made by rubbing wings, abdomen and/or legs together.

**Similar insects:** Crickets and katydids have antennae of less than 30 segments. Ears, when present, on base of abdomen.

STEVE PARISH

 **HABITAT** BUSHES & GRASSES

 **FOOD** LEAVES, GRASS

Order *Orthoptera* (continued)

**Length:** 5–100 cm

**Identification:** As for other Orthoptera (p. 14). **Crickets** and **katydids** have antennae of more than 30 segments, half to several times the body length. Female crickets and katydids have a long, thin egg-laying ovipositor (see photo at right of cricket). Burrowing mole crickets have strong digging forelegs. Male king crickets have huge biting mouthparts. There are 1806 spp. in Australia.

JIRI LOCHMAN

**Where found:** In vegetation, at all heights from ground. Also on the ground, in burrows and in buildings.

**Life history:** Male makes loud call which attracts female. After mating, female digs into soil or vegetation with her ovipositor, then lays eggs. Nymph may take 10 moults to become adult.

**Habits:** Active day and night, feed on plants and animals.

**Notes:** Songs are longer and more complex than those of grasshoppers. Katydids call from amongst leaves and most crickets call from ground.

**Similar insects:** Grasshoppers and locusts have antennae of more than 30 segments. Ears, when present, are on front legs.

**HABITAT**
TREES, BUSHES
& GROUND

**FOOD**
PLANTS,
ANIMALS

# earwigs

Order *Dermaptera* (= leathery wings)

D. KNOWLES

**Length:** 5–55 mm

**Aust. spp.:** 63

**Identification:** Small to large, shiny, flat-bodied crawling insects, usually brown or black in colour. At end of abdomen are pincers, heavier and more curved in male. May be wingless. When present, forewings cover only thorax, hindwings fold to fit beneath them. Head bears threadlike antennae, chewing mouthparts, compound eyes.

**Where found:** In damp places under bark, stones, logs. Common in gardens.

**Life history:** Female lays 15–80 eggs in a burrow or hole, then guards them, removes fungi from them for 2–3 weeks, until they hatch. She stays with the young until they have moulted twice. Young stages look like adults, but only develop wings after they have moulted 3 or 4 times.

**Habits:** Eat vegetable matter, dead insects, some live prey. Pincers used for defence and sometimes to capture prey.

**Notes:** "Earwig" comes from ear-shaped hindwings. Introduced European Earwig is a pest in gardens. Painted Earwig (see photo) is a flat-bodied native species which lives under bark.

**Similar insects:** None.

**HABITAT**
UNDER LOGS,
ROCKS

**FOOD**
PLANTS,
INSECTS

# stick and leaf insects

Order *Phasmatodea* (= like a ghost)

**Length:** 30–300 mm

**Aust. spp.:** 150

**Identification:** Medium to large plant-eating insects, with long, round or flattened bodies, and long legs. Colour, pattern and body form resemble sticks, leaves, grasses. Small head bears compound eyes, chewing mouthparts. Sometimes both sexes wingless, or female lacks wings. Small forewing does not quite cover gauzy hindwing. Legs may carry spines, can be held along body.

**Where found:** On leaves or branches; some spp. on grasses or leaf litter.

**Life history:** Female drops 100–1000 eggs onto ground. Some hatch on ground, others are taken underground by ants and hatch in their nests. Nymphs moult 5–8 times before becoming adult.

**Habits:** Most move about only at night, feeding on plants.

**Notes:** Seedlike egg bears a knob which attracts ants. Females of some spp. lay eggs without mating.

**Similar insects:** Mantids have large triangular heads, huge eyes, prey-grasping forelegs.

M & I MORCOMBE

**HABITAT** TREES & GRASSES

**FOOD** PLANTS

Order *Hemiptera* (= half-wings)

**Length:** 1–110 mm

**Aust. spp.in order Hemiptera (pp. 18, 19):** 5650

**Identification:** Order Hemiptera includes tiny to very large insects whose mouthparts form a long, sharply pointed beak for sucking up food. The antennae are made up of no more than five segments. **True bugs** have rounded or flat forewings which are hard at the base, gauzy at the tip, and hide the membranous hindwings. There are 2705 spp. of true bugs in Australia.

D. KNOWLES

**Where found:** Where food is available.

**Life history:** True bug nymphs are shaped like wingless adults, though colours and markings may be different.

**Habits:** Usually feed on plant juices. Some, like assassin bugs, eat other animals. Some, like blood-sucking bed bugs, are parasites.

**Notes:** Assassin bugs, shield bugs, stink bugs, jewel bugs (see photo), bed bugs and water bugs are all true bugs.

**Similar insects:** Beetles have stiff forewings which meet in centre and cover hindwings. Cockroaches have very long, many-segmented antennae.

**HABITAT**
IN ALMOST
ALL HABITATS

**FOOD**
PLANT JUICES,
OTHER FLUIDS

Order *Hemiptera* (continued)

**Length:** Up to 70 mm

**Identification:** As for other Hemiptera. **Cicadas** are small to large bugs, whose heads point down and backwards, so their beaks seem to come from between their front legs. Each antenna consists of a base segment and a thin bristle. The forewings rise to a peak over the hindwings. There are 252 spp. of cicadas in Australia.

**Where found:** Adults in trees and grasses.

**Life history:** To attract females, male vibrates drumlike membranes on abdomen. After mating, female lays eggs on a tree branch or plant stem. Nymphs hatch, fall to the ground, dig in with their front legs, then remain underground for 9 months to several years before emerging, climbing trees and moulting into adults (see photo).

**Habits:** Nymphs feed on weak

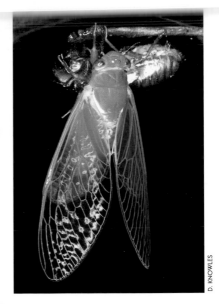

D. KNOWLES

sap from tree roots, so may take many years to become adults. Adults feed on sap from branches in treetops.

**Notes:** Cicadas belong to a group of bugs with forewings held roof-like, which includes treehoppers and leafhoppers.

**Similar insects:** None.

**HABITAT**
ADULT IN
TREES

**FOOD**
PLANT
JUICES

# lacewings and ant-lions

Order *Neuroptera* (= net-veined wings)

PETER SLATER

**Wingspan:** 5–150 mm

**Aust. spp.:** 623

**Identification:** Small to large insects with two pairs of equal-sized, lacy wings with forked veins at tips, usually held roof-like when resting. Head bears threadlike antennae, chewing mouthparts, and large eyes. Larvae are wingless predators with mouthparts drawn out into piercing, sucking tubes.

**Where found:** Most habitats.

**Life history:** Ant-lion eggs scattered on sand; lacewing eggs laid on stalks. Larvae suck juices of prey. After 3–5 moults, they spin silken cocoons, pupate and emerge as winged adults (photo left). Life cycle 6 months to 2 years.

**Habits:** Lacewing adults (photo left) eat soft-bodied insects such as aphids.

**Notes:** Ant-lion larvae (photo below) dig pits in sand, lie in wait at the bottom, seize insects falling in.

**Similar insects:** Alderflies, dobsonflies lack forked veins on wingtips; stoneflies hold wings flat; caddis flies have fewer cross veins in wings.

JIRI LOCHMAN

**HABITAT**
ALL SORTS
OF HABITATS

**FOOD**
INSECTS

# beetles

Order *Coleoptera* (= sheath wings)

**Length:** 0.4–80 mm

**Aust. spp.:** 28 200

**Identification:** Tiny to large insects. Hard wingcases do not beat in flight and at rest meet down the middle of the abdomen, hiding gauzy hindwings. Head bears antennae, compound eyes, chewing mouthparts. First segment of thorax is enlarged.

**Where found:** In burrows in earth, tunnels in wood, on foliage, in animal dung, in water and elsewhere.

STANLEY BREEDEN

**Life history:** Female lays eggs on or near a food supply. Male and female may work together to provide larvae with food (plant, dung or a dead animal). Larva has hard head, chewing mouthparts, and usually has legs. After several instars, larva becomes pupa and finally emerges as adult. Life cycle may vary from several weeks to several years.

**Habits:** Larval foods include fungi, dung, rotting wood, carrion, other insects. Adults include predators, scavengers[G] and herbivores[G].

**Notes:** Coleoptera is the largest order of insects, with over 300 000 spp. worldwide.

**Similar insects:** Bugs have sucking beaks. Cockroaches lack hard wingcases.

**HABITAT**
IN ALMOST
ALL HABITATS

**FOOD**
PLANTS &
ANIMALS

# flies

Order *Diptera* (= two wings)

JIRI LOCHMAN

**Wingspan:** Up to 50 mm

**Aust. spp. in order Diptera (pp. 22, 23):** 7786

**Identification:** Diptera includes flies, mosquitoes, midges, sandflies etc. They are tiny to large insects with gauzy forewings, whose hindwings are reduced to stalked knobs. The large, movable head bears antennae, large compound eyes, sucking, and sometimes piercing, mouthparts. Legs are often long.

**Where found:** In almost all habitats.

**Life history:** Many fly spp. mate on the wing. Eggs are laid near or on moist larval food. They hatch quickly into pale, legless maggots, with small heads and chewing mouthparts, which may swim in their food. Some larvae are parasites. After 3–4 instars, the larva becomes a pupa. Life history of many spp. may take less than one week.

**Habits:** Many adult flies are active during day, but some fly at night. Larvae of most spp. feed on rotting animal or vegetable matter. Many adult flies salivate on food, then suck up partly digested slush.

**Notes:** Some spp. carry disease organisms, depositing these with saliva, or with the feet. Some inject them when sucking blood.

**Similar insects:** Only flies have stalked knobs instead of hindwings.

**HABITAT**
IN ALMOST
ALL HABITATS

**FOOD**
PLANTS &
ANIMALS

Order *Diptera* (continued)

**Length:** To about 15 mm

**Identification:** As for other Diptera. **Mosquitoes** have long, narrow wings whose veins and rear edges bear scales. The mouthparts are used for piercing and sucking and the male mosquito usually has feathery antennae. There are 275 spp. of mosquitoes in Australia.

**Where found:** Near water, especially in warmer climates.

**Life history:** Male's feathery antennae detect high-pitched whine of female's wings. After mating and usually feeding on blood (see photo), female lays her eggs in water. Here they hatch into larvae, then develop into active pupae, before emerging as adults.

**Habits:** Only the female feeds on blood; males suck sap or nectar. Different spp. feed at different times of day. Females feed from a variety of animals.

**Notes:** Females of some spp. of mosquitoes carry organisms causing human diseases such as Ross River virus, dengue fever and malaria. Mosquito larvae can grow and pupate in small amounts of water.

**Similar insects:** Midges (wingspan 1–8 mm) do not "bite". Sandflies (wingspan less than 5 mm) "bite".

PETER MARSACK

**HABITAT** NEAR FRESH, SALTY WATER

**FOOD** BLOOD, PLANT JUICES

# moths

Order *Lepidoptera* (= scaly wings)

D. KNOWLES

**Length:** 3–250 mm

**Aust. spp. in order Lepidoptera (pp. 24, 25):** 20 816

**Identification:** Small to very large insects, whose bodies and wings are covered by tiny, overlapping scales. Head bears antennae (feathery in some male moths), large compound eyes, and mouthparts which form a tube to suck up food. **Moths** usually hold their wings flat at rest. Their fore- and hindwings are usually coupled by a spine and hook.

**Where found:** Most habitats.

**Life history:** Male uses antennae to locate female by scent. Female lays eggs on food plant. Caterpillar has hard head, soft thorax bearing 3 pairs of jointed true legs, abdomen bearing fleshy false legs. After 4–5 instars, pupates, sometimes in silken cocoon, usually in sheltered place, then emerges as adult.

**Habits:** Active at night (a few by day). Most feed on nectar.

**Notes:** Hercules Moth (adult above left, caterpillar below) is Australia's largest moth, with 250 mm wingspan.

**Similar insects:** Butterflies rest with wings upright.

STAN FY BREEDEN

**HABITAT** IN ALMOST ALL HABITATS

**FOOD** PLANTS, NECTAR

236

Red-eye Skipper Butterfly

Cave Moth

Emperor Gum Moth

Zodiac Moth

*Cardamyla carinentalis*

underside of *Vindula arsinoe*

Common Eggfly Butterfly (male)

Red Lacewing Butterfly

Cairns Birdwing Butterfly (male)

Common Eggfly Butterfly (female)

underside of Cairns Birdwing (male)

Orchard Swallowtail Butterfly

Order *Lepidoptera* (continued)

**Wingspan:** 3–250 mm

**Identification:** As for other Lepidoptera. Australia's approximately 400 spp. of **butterflies** usually have club-ended antennae. Wings are not coupled together; most spp. rest with wings upright (photo above shows the wings fanning). One group, the Skippers, sits with only the forewings upright and the hindwings flat.

**Where found:** Most habitats.

**Life history:** Female lays eggs on a selected food plant. Caterpillar hatches, feeds, moults 4–5 times, changes to a pupa or chrysalis⁶, then emerges as adult.

**Habits:** Active during day or early evening. Butterflies feed on nectar and other liquids.

**Notes:** Most spectacular Aust. spp. are members of the swallowtail family, to which the Ulysses Butterfly (above) and the large Cape York Birdwing (wingspan up to 140 mm) belong. Other families include whites, browns and blues.

**Similar insects:** Moths rest with wings flat; very few moths have clubbed antennae.

HABITAT
IN ALMOST
ALL HABITATS

FOOD
NECTAR
& FLUIDS

# scorpion flies

Order *Mecoptera* (= long wings)

**Wingspan:** Up to 50 mm

**Aust. spp.:** 28

**Identification:** Small to medium-sized flying insects with long, thin legs. Long head bears threadlike antennae, large eyes and chewing mouthparts. The two pairs of gauzy, veined wings are almost equal in size.

**Where found:** Southwestern WA and eastern Australia.

**Life history:** Courting male of some spp. catches an insect and gives it to female, who eats it (see photo). Female lays eggs on ground or in a hole in loose soil. Larvae are like caterpillars with short legs and large jaws. They live in damp situations such as leaf litter or moss and eat dead insects and plants.

**Habits:** Adult scorpion flies feed in various ways. Predators hang from vegetation by their forelegs and catch passing insects with their long, clawed hindlegs.

**Notes:** Name comes from shape of male abdomen, which may be curled forward at end like "tail" of scorpion. One Tas. species feeds on moss and remains active in snow.

**Similar insects:** True flies have only one pair of wings.

**HABITAT**
DAMP
SITUATIONS

**FOOD**
INSECTS

# ants

Order *Hymenoptera* (= membrane wings)

**Length (Hymenoptera generally):** 0.15–120 mm

**Aust. spp. in order Hymenoptera (pp. 27–30):** 14 781

**Aust. spp. of ants:** 4 000

**Identification:** Hymenoptera includes ants, wasps, bees and sawflies, tiny to large insects, most with a waist between the first two segments of the abdomen. Those with wings have two membranous pairs, forewings larger than hindwings and coupled to them with hooks. Head bears short to long antennae, large compound eyes and chewing mouthparts. In some groups, the ovipositor has become a sting. **Ants** have the first segment of the abdomen fused to the thorax and a waist between the second and third segments. Their antennae have angled "elbows".

**Where found:** Most habitats, especially warmer areas.

**Life history:** Winged males and females fly from nest and mate. Males die, females shed wings and begin colonies. The larvae are legless.

**Habits:** In an ant colony are up to 1 million individuals — infertile workers and soldiers, and fertile females and males.

**Notes:** Adult ants eat liquids. Some care for and "milk" caterpillars and aphids.

**Similar insects:** Some other insects and spiders mimic ants, but lack double waist and elbowed antennae.

JIRI LOCHMAN

**HABITAT IN ALMOST ALL HABITATS**

**FOOD PLANTS & ANIMALS**

# bees

**Identification:** As for other Hymenoptera. **Bees** have branched body hairs, and the hindleg or abdomen usually has a "basket", or special hairs for carrying pollen (photo right). Mouthparts form "tongue" for getting nectar. There are around 1600 spp. of bees in Australia.

**Where found:** Adults visit flowers (see photo right).

**Life history:** In many spp. females store sperm, then lay eggs when food is available. An egg is laid in a cell stocked with nectar and pollen as larval food. Hive<sup>G</sup> bee workers feed the legless larvae. After pupating, the adult emerges.

JIRI LOCHMAN

**Habits:** Most spp. are solitary, each female digging a nest in the ground (photo below left) or in wood, and placing in it pollen and nectar for her larvae. A few bees live in hives consisting of workers, queens (females) and drones (males).

**Notes:** Aust. spp. include native, stingless hive bees, and introduced, stinging Honey Bee.

**Similar insects:** Some flies and wasps resemble bees, but lack pollen baskets and branched hairs on bodies.

**HABITAT**
IN ALMOST
ALL HABITATS

**FOOD**
NECTAR &
POLLEN

Order *Hymenoptera* (continued)

**Identification:** As for other Hymenoptera. **Wasps** include groups whose larvae parasitise insects and spiders. Eggs, young stages or adults may serve as hosts for the wasp larvae to consume.

**Where found:** Most habitats.

**Life history:** The female of some groups searches for hosts for her larvae, stings them to paralyse them, then carries them to a prepared burrow or mud cell (see photo) and lays an egg on each. When the legless wasp larva hatches, it eats the host before pupating and later emerging as an adult wasp. In other groups, the egg is laid in, or on, a free-living host.

RAOUL SLATER

**Habits:** Adults feed on nectar or other fluids and, like bees, may carry pollen between flowers. Larvae feed on plants or arthropods. Female of one group uses a pebble to firm down loose soil above her nest.

**Notes:** Cuckoo wasps lay their eggs in the nests of other spp., and their larvae eat the wasp larvae and the hosts as well.

**Similar insects:** Bees store nectar and pollen as food for their larvae and have pollen-gathering leg baskets and branched body hairs.

HABITAT
IN ALMOST
ALL HABITATS

FOOD
ADULTS EAT
NECTAR

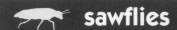 

Order *Hymenoptera* (continued)

JIRI LOCHMAN

**Length:** 3–55 mm

**Identification:** As for other Hymenoptera. **Sawflies** are small to large Hymenoptera, which do not have a waist. Female's ovipositor has sawlike tip. Larvae have legs on thorax and false legs on abdomen.

**Where found:** Most habitats.

**Life history:** Female lays eggs into slits cut into plant with her ovipositor. Some larvae bore into wood or mine leaves, but most live on foliage. Larvae may pupate in the soil.

**Habits:** One family of sawflies is parasitic, using beetle larvae as hosts. Larvae, which feed on leaf surfaces (see photo right),

may cling together and wave abdomens when molested. Larvae of some spp. "spit" nasty liquid at predators. Adults eat nectar.

**Notes:** Aust. has 176 spp. of sawflies, including introduced European Sirex Wasp, which kills pine trees by introducing fungus into their tissues.

**Similar insects:** Moth or butterfly caterpillars never have more than 5 pairs of false legs, while sawflies have six or more. Bees, winged ants and wasps have waists and may sting. Sawflies do not sting.

 **HABITAT**
LEAVES &
FLOWERS

 **FOOD**
NECTAR &
LEAVES

# Some introduced insects

**Honey bees:** are useful to humans, for they produce honey. Here a bee-keeper tends his hives.

**Cockroach:** 2 introduced spp. live in houses, where they eat and foul food. Also found in sewers.

**Rice weevil:** larva lives inside a grain, eating it out until only the husk remains. Pest in stored grain.

**Silverfish:** feeds upon wallpaper, book covers and fabrics and is a pest in homes, shops and libraries.

The **Wanderer Butterfly** (above right) probably introduced itself many times. However, the species was not established until the 1870s, when humans brought the plants on which its caterpillar (above left) feeds.

# Spiders

An animal is a spider if it:

* has 2 body sections –
  cephalothorax and abdomen
* has 4 pairs of walking legs
* has fangs
* has simple eyes
* has book-lungs<sup>G</sup>
* lacks antennae
* is wingless

Golden Orb-weaver

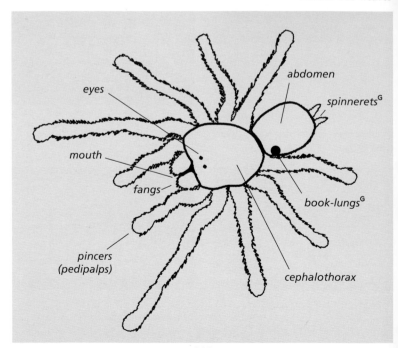

# Spider groups

All spiders are classed as Araneae. Australian spiders can be further grouped into primitive or modern families.

| PRIMITIVE SPIDERS 10 families | MODERN SPIDERS 59 families |
| --- | --- |
| Have fangs that move up and down, like pickaxes | Have fangs that move side-to-side, like pincers |
| Venom<sup>G</sup> glands in bases of chelicerae | Venom glands in head |
| Two pairs of spinnerets | Usually three pairs of spinnerets |
| No spinning plate | May have a spinning-plate |
| Breathe through two pairs of book-lungs | Breathe through one pair of book-lungs and tracheae |
| Use silk for egg sacs, and triplines, to line burrows and occasionally to weave catching webs | Use silk for egg sacs, to build shelters of various kinds and to weave catching webs |

## Be aware

These Australian spiders have venom that can harm humans:

* Sydney Funnel-web
* Blue Mountains Funnel-web
* Northern Tree Funnel-web
* White-tailed Spider
* Mouse Spider
* Black House Spider
* Red-back Spider

Wolf Spider

IAN MORRIS

# trapdoor spiders

Families *Idiopidae* (= same eyes) and *Ctenizidae*

M & I MORCOMBE

**Body length:** ♀ to 40 ♂ to 25 mm

**Identification:** Medium to large, ground-living, burrowing spiders. Usually dark-coloured, sometimes mottled; male may be brighter. Large, downwards-moving chelicerae. Two pairs of book-lungs. Four spinnerets, the final segment of the last pair short and rounded.

**Where found:** In a variety of habitats, including rainforest and desert.

**Habits:** Burrows may, or may not be sealed by a lid or "trapdoor" of silk and earth. A burrow may be more than 1 m in length and dug at an angle or straight down. Spider waits inside burrow (see photo), then seizes insects or other small creatures passing by. Males wander in search of females in summer, usually in damp weather.

**Notes:** Much less aggressive than funnel-webs. When in danger, will usually "freeze" with legs close to body, lie upside down, or run away.

**Similar spiders:** Funnel-webs live in silken tubes without doors and with lines of silk running from entrance. They are usually darker, solid colours, and when threatened they fight back.

**HABITAT**
ON GROUND &
IN BURROWS

**FOOD**
SMALL
CREATURES

# funnel-web spiders

Family *Hexathelidae* (= six spinnerets)

**Body length:** ♀ up to 30 ♂ smaller

**Identification:** Large to very large, ground- or tree-living spiders. Blue-black, purple-black or dark grey in colour. Cephalothorax bears massive, downwards-moving chelicerae, 8 eyes, long, leg-like pedipalps. Underside of abdomen has 2 pairs of book-lungs, usually 6, sometimes 4, spinnerets. Final segment of longest spinneret is longer than it is wide.

D. KNOWLES

**Where found:** From eastern Qld south to Tas. and southwest to Mt Lofty Ranges, SA. Home is long, flat tube of silk, placed in rock crevice, crack in tree, or in a burrow. Mature male leaves refuge to wander in search of female.

**Habits:** Spider sits at entrance to tube at night. Silk strands from entrance warn of approaching prey, or danger. Female lays eggs in brood chamber and young spiders remain there for some time.

**Notes:** To bite, raises front of body and front legs off ground. Venom can be fatal to humans. If bitten, apply pressure bandage and seek medical help. Antivenom[6] is available.

**Similar spiders:** Trapdoor spiders are often mottled in colour and when in danger may "freeze" or flee.

**HABITAT**
MOIST
HABITATS

**FOOD**
SMALL
CREATURES

# huntsman spiders

Family *Heteropodidae* (= different legs)

**Body length:** ♀ to 47 ♂ to 30 mm

**Leg-span:** 160 mm

**Known Aust. spp.:** 93

**Identification:** Medium to large, climbing spiders with flattened brown or grey bodies, sometimes banded legs. Eyes in 2 rows: 4 back, 4 front. Oval-shaped abdomen. All 4 pairs of long, hairy legs are spread sideways, so a huntsman spider can scuttle sideways. Male has smaller body, longer legs than female.

**Where found:** In forests and woodlands, under bark, or flakes of rock, in houses.

**Habits:** Active at night, especially on trees, running down or leaping on small creatures. Female remains with white, papery egg-sac, then opens it to allow young to escape. They stay with her for some time.

**Notes:** Most not harmful to humans. Hair tufts on ends of legs help movement on vertical surfaces. Spider in photo has just shed its outgrown skin.

**Similar spiders:** Only large spiders with legs spread sideways. Crab spiders have spread legs also, but are smaller.

RAOUL SLATER

**HABITAT**
TREES, ROCKS
& HOUSES

**FOOD**
SMALL
CREATURES

# whistling spiders

Family *Theraphosidae*

**Body length:** up to 60 mm

**Leg-span:** up to 160 mm

**Identification:** Large to very large, ground-living or burrowing spiders. Body and legs, or legs only, covered with fine, velvety hairs. Legs end in claws and tufts of hairs or brushes (sometimes called brush-footed spiders). Large, downwards-moving chelicerae, two pairs of book-lungs. Four spinnerets.

**Where found:** Most habitats.

**Habits:** Group includes the huge bird-eating spiders, whose prey is insects, ground birds, reptiles and frogs. These spiders "whistle" by rubbing spines on the bases of their pedipalps over bristles on their chelicerae. Females of some spp. hold their egg sacs. After hatching, young spiders remain in the burrow for some time.

**Notes:** Some spp. survive flooding by taking refuge in an airlock formed in a side chamber to the burrow shaft. Sometimes this can be closed with a trapdoor.

**Similar spiders:** None covered with velvety hair.

M & I MORCOMBE

**HABITAT**
ON GROUND &
IN BURROWS

**FOOD**
SMALL
CREATURES

# ✳ lynx spiders

Family *Oxyopidae* (= sharp eyes)

**Length:** up to 10 mm

**Identification:** Spiders with tapering abdomens and long, thin legs covered with long spines. Head is high in front and bears 8 eyes, set in 4 rows of 2. Often colourful (light green, brown or yellow), with light and dark bands along sides of abdomen.

**Where found:** In trees, grass or low vegetation.

**Habits:** Usually seen on sunny days, moving actively about on leaves and branches, hunting for small insects, which they stalk then pounce upon. White egg-sac is placed in leaves tied together with silk, then guarded by female.

D. KNOWLES

**Notes:** As wind sways leaves, lynx spider sways on its slender legs. Does not make shelter. Name comes from pouncing, cat-like habits.

**Similar spiders:** Other tree-living spiders lack colours and long, slender, very spiny legs.

**HABITAT**
BUSHES,
TREES, GRASS

**FOOD**
SMALL
INSECTS

# wolf spiders

Family *Lycosidae* (after Lycaon, whom Jupiter turned into a wolf)

**Length:** ♀ to 16 ♂ to 13 mm

**Known Aust. spp.:** 130

**Identification:** Small to very large, long-legged, ground-living spiders. Grey or brown body, with carapace<sup>G</sup> often patterned in a sunburst of grey, brown or orange. Carapace is high in front. Eyes are in 3 rows: 2 back, 2 centre, 4 front.

**Where found:** Most habitats, especially near water in open woodland, grassland and mallee, almost always on ground.

**Habits:** Many spp. make a burrow, which may have a lid, or a collar of silk, or a sheet-web around it. Many shelter in crevices.

All leave home to search for prey. Female carries her egg sac attached to her spinnerets.

**Notes:** After young hatch, female carries them around on her abdomen (see photo). Finally, they climb grass blades, spin strands of silk and "balloon" away to new places.

**Similar spiders:** Huntsman spiders climb, have eyes in two rows: 4 back, 4 front.

M & I MORCOMBE

**HABITAT**
ON GROUND,
ALL AUST.

**FOOD**
SMALL
CREATURES

# comb-footed spiders

Family *Theridiidae*

JIRI LOCHMAN

**Length:** Red-back Spider (above) ♀ 6–11 ♂ 3 mm

**Aust. spp. in family Theridiidae:** about 90

**Identification:** Small to medium-sized, web-spinning spiders, having a comb with toothed spines on each hindleg. Abdomen often globe-shaped. **Red-back Spider** female, which can harm humans, is black or nearly so, with red markings on top and underside of abdomen.

**Where found:** Red-back Spider in dry habitats (often in buildings or rubbish).

**Habits:** Red-back rests upside-down in silk retreat during day, emerges onto web at night. Web is a tangle of threads from which hang several gummy threads fastened to ground or other surface. A crawling insect brushes a thread, is caught and its struggles break the thread, which snaps upwards. The spider dashes from its shelter, bites the victim, then wraps it in silk and sucks it dry.

**Notes:** Comb on hindlegs is used to rake out silk into wide ribbons as it leaves spinnerets when wrapping prey. Anyone bitten by a Red-back Spider should rest and be taken to a hospital. Antivenom will be given if necessary.

**Similar spiders:** Red-back has red on top and underside of abdomen. Young Red-backs may be grey, or black and white.

**HABITAT**
PLANTS &
BUILDINGS

**FOOD**
INSECTS

# jumping spiders

Family *Salticidae* (*salto* = to dance, leap, spring)

**Length:** up to 12 mm

**Aust. spp.:** 252

**Identification:** Small to medium-sized, often colourful spiders, capable of long, high jumps to secure prey or escape danger. Front of cephalothorax upright. Eyes are in 3 rows: 2 back, 2 centre, 4 front, with middle front pair large. Pedipalps may be furry and white. Legs short, strong; abdomen usually longer than wide.

D. KNOWLES

**Where found:** On vegetation.

**Habits:** Daytime hunters, which move in leaps and dashes. When alert, these spiders constantly move the cephalothorax to look around and may appear to watch a human observer. Like all spiders, they trail safety lines. Courting males wave their pedipalps and move to display body colours and patterns (see photo). Female remains with white egg-sac in silk shelter.

**Notes:** Greatest variety of jumping spiders in tropics. Some mimic insects such as ants in shape. Some can see prey at 20 cm and jump 18 cm.

**Similar spiders:** None matches eye formation, jerky movement and leaping ability.

**HABITAT**
TREES &
BUSHES

**FOOD**
INSECTS

# net-casting spiders

Family *Deinopidae* (= evil eyes)

D. KNOWLES

**Length:** ♀ up to 25
♂ up to 12 mm

**Aust. spp.:** 14

**Identification:** Medium to large-sized spiders with long bodies, and very long legs with large joints. Mottled brown or grey in colour. Eyes in 3 rows: 2 back, 2 largest centre, 4 front. Uses a spinning plate to produce sticky, elastic silk for a catching net.

**Where found:** Most common in eucalypt forests, especially in southeast.

**Habits:** During day hangs down on silk thread, looking like stick. At night, weaves postage-stamp-sized net, holds it in front legs, then flings it over passing prey. Prey is bitten, bundled up and sucked dry. Egg-sacs are attached to rocks or low plants, then guarded by female.

**Notes:** Also called stick spiders or ogre-faced spiders. Net may be used more than once if undamaged, eaten if damaged, or discarded.

**Similar spiders:** None.

HABITAT
FORESTS &
GARDENS

FOOD
INSECTS

# laceweb spiders

Family *Amaurobiidae*

Spinning plate produces lacy silken threads, making webs easy to see. **Black House Spider** is coal-black, with stout build.

**Where found:** Hides in crevices in window corners, rafters, rockeries, stone walls, outdoor light fittings.

**Habits:** Female never leaves retreat and web, rushing out to seize creatures caught in its blue-white silk. Mature male roams, courts female by plucking web, may remain with her after mating. White egg sacs are guarded by female. Young float away on silken threads.

**Notes:** Black House Spider weaves funnel-shaped web, is timid. Bite can cause pain and sickness to humans.

**Similar spiders:** Funnel-webs larger, with purplish abdomen, shiny cephalothorax. Their webs do not form funnels.

**Length:** Black House Spider (above) ♀ up to 18 ♂ 9 mm

**Aust. spp. in family Amaurobiidae:** about 20

**Identification:** Small to medium-sized, grey to black spiders which spin funnel-shaped webs near a crack or crevice (like a window-corner) in which the spider takes refuge. Eyes in 2 rows: 4 back, 4 front. Abdomen egg-shaped.

**HABITAT**
ROCKS,
BUILDINGS

**FOOD**
INSECTS

**triangular spiders**

Family *Araneidae* (continued)

**Length:** ♀ up to 10 mm

**Aust. spp.:** 9

**Identification:** Small spiders with cephalothorax and triangular abdomen brightly coloured (green, yellow, orange, red, white) and glossy. Two front pairs of legs are long and spiny, and used to grip prey. Two hind pairs are short, and used to hold spider in place on leaf or bark.

**Where found:** In forests, especially on bushfire regrowth, on trees and ferns.

**Habits:** During day, sits on a leaf, holding on with hind pairs of legs, front pairs of legs outstretched, seizing passing insects. At night, may hang from a thread, grabbing prey with front legs. The globe-shaped, pink-orange egg-sac hangs under leaf.

**Notes:** These spiders are probably related to orb-web weavers. They weave reduced webs, use silk for safety lines, egg-sacs and prey-wrapping. Bright colours blend with foliage and bark, and serve as camouflage.

**Similar spiders:** None.

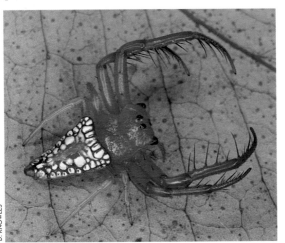

D. KNOWLES

 **HABITAT** FORESTS & WOODLANDS

 **FOOD** INSECTS

# crab spiders

Family *Thomisidae*

**Length:** ♀ up to 15 mm, ♂ smaller

**Identification:** Small spiders, crablike in shape, whose front two pairs of legs are strong and spiny. They have 8 eyes: 4 back, 4 front, sometimes on turrets. Some crab spiders have upper surface colour and texture of bark. Others, known as flower spiders (photo above), are smooth and coloured white, yellow, green, red.

D. KNOWLES

**Where found:** Most spp. live in warmer climates.

**Habits:** Crab and flower spiders wait in ambush during day. Flower spiders sit within flowers of the same colour, anchored by their hind legs, front legs and pedipalps ready to seize a visiting insect. Silk shelter made for woolly egg sacs, which are guarded by female until eggs hatch.

**Notes:** May catch insects many times larger than themselves, especially butterflies. A flower spider "owns" its flower and remains there until it wilts.

**Similar spiders:** None.

**HABITAT** BARK & FLOWERS

**FOOD** INSECTS

# bolas spiders

Family *Araneidae* (from the Latin *aranea* = spider)

STANLEY BREEDEN

**Length:** ♀ 14 (when pregnant) ♂ up to 1.5 mm

**Aust. spp.:** 4

**Identification:** Small to medium-size spiders with small cephalothorax, large plump abdomen and short, strong, legs. Body and legs are covered with fine hairs.

**Where found:** In dry or wet eucalypt forests and in gardens. Lives in foliage.

**Habits:** At night, spider hangs from several strands of strong silk. Moths are captured on a thread ending in a sticky blob, the bolas, whirled by a second leg. There is evidence to show that the spider gives out an odour similar to that of a female moth. (Species shown in photo is the Magnificent Spider.) Spindle-shaped egg-sacs are guarded by the female.

**Notes:** Australia's 4 spp. of bolas spiders are related to orb-web weaving spiders, but no longer weave webs. A moth may be "played" like a fish on a line until it can be reeled in and bitten. Harmless to humans.

**Similar spiders:** None.

**HABITAT**
FORESTS &
GARDENS

**FOOD**
FLYING
INSECTS

Family *Araneidae* (continued)

**Length:** ♀ 12 (to 20 while pregnant) ♂ 3 mm

**Aust. spp.:** 7

**Identification:** A small to medium-sized spider with a bumpy abdomen coloured black, white and brown and patterned to mimic bird-dropping. Legs are banded and held close to body during day.

D. KNOWLES

**Where found:** Usually in bushes and trees.

**Habits:** During day, sits huddled on leaf in open, overlooked by predators. At night hangs head down with front two pairs of legs outstretched. Attracts male moths by giving out scent like that of female moth, seizes, bites, wraps and eats them. Female most often seen when guarding group of round, brown egg-sacs (see photo).

**Notes:** Bird-dropping spiders are also called death's head spiders. Young bird-dropping spider builds orb web to catch prey, but when adult takes to ambushing victims attracted by scent lure.

**Similar spiders:** Some crab spiders have knobby, dull-coloured upper surfaces, but their legs fan out sideways and front two pairs carry spines.

**HABITAT**
BUSHES & TREES

**FOOD**
INSECTS

Family *Araneidae* (continued)

**Length:** ♀ up to 15 ♂ 5 mm

**Identification:** Medium-sized spider which rests on cross of thickened silk in web, appearing to have only 4 legs. Female's abdomen is striped yellow, red, black and white. The legs are banded. Male is plain red-brown.

**Where found:** In foliage, usually within 1–2 m of ground, often near water.

**Habits:** Active during day, repairing web if damaged by large victim. Prey caught in web is bitten, turned by third, shorter pair of legs as it is wrapped in silk, then sucked dry. Grey-green or brown, pear-shaped egg sacs are attached to foliage near web.

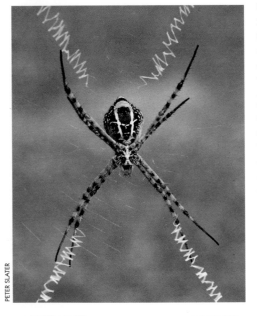

PETER SLATER

**Notes:** Cross on web consists of two ribbons of lacy, zig-zagged silk which intersect at the centre of the web, and on which spider rests. Cross adds strength to web. When threatened, spider may grip web and shake it.

**Similar spiders:** None has a complete cross on its web.

**HABITAT** TREES OFTEN NEAR WATER

**FOOD** INSECTS

Family *Araneidae* (continued)

**Length:** ♀ up to 45 ♂ 6 mm

**Identification:** A large to very large spider with long legs. Female has plum-coloured body with silver-grey sheen, and legs banded black, yellow and orange. Male is brown and tiny compared to female. Female builds a large web of strong golden silk with a section not filled in at top.

**Where found:** In woodlands, forests, gardens, shrubs, road verges, between power lines and fence wires.

**Habits:** Huge web is anchored to trees, wires or poles. Orb part of web may be more than 1 m across, with anchor-strands on either side. Above and at the sides are tangles of threads (photo shows female in one of these areas).

Female remains in web night and day, repairs it if torn.

**Notes:** Smaller Quicksilver Spiders may share the web. Bite of Golden Orb-weaver is harmless to humans.

**Similar spiders:** None with large golden web.

STANLEY BREEDEN

**HABITAT** GARDENS, WOODLANDS

**FOOD** SMALL CREATURES

# jewel spiders

Family *Araneidae* (continued)

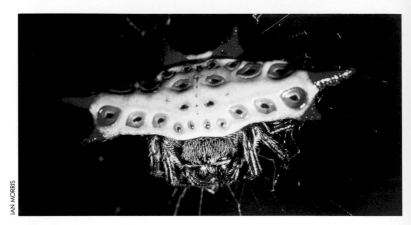

IAN MORRIS

**Length:** up to 8 mm

**Identification:** Small, brightly-coloured, short-legged spiders. The broad, hard, shield-like abdomen has up to 6 spines around its edges.

**Where found:** Most habitats, especially tropical and temperate areas, in woodlands and shrublands, often near water.

**Habits:** Upright orb web has very close threads, and may be placed alone or in a group of other webs. The threads supporting the web carry tufts of fluffy white silk.

**Notes:** Best known jewel spider is the Christmas Spider, whose female is black, orange and cream, with a six-pointed abdomen. The male, which is only 3 mm long, has blunt spines. Jewel spiders are harmless to humans.

**Similar spiders:** Two-spined Spider has two large yellowish spines and a soft abdomen.

**HABITAT** BUSHES & TREES

**FOOD** SMALL INSECTS

264

# garden spiders

Family *Araneidae* (continued)

**Length:** ♀ up to 30 when pregnant ♂ up to 20 mm

**Aust. spp.:** More than 100

**Identification:** Medium-sized, heavily built, hairy spiders, with a hump on each "shoulder" of the plump abdomen. Colour usually grey or brown. Outstretched legs show shiny red-brown sections.

JIRI LOCHMAN

**Where found:** In many habitats, including gardens. Webs are made across open spaces above tracks, streams.

**Habits:** Hangs head down in orb web at night (see photo). Tears down much of web at dawn, remakes it the following evening. During day, hides in foliage near web site, legs tucked close to body. Fluffy, yellow or golden egg sac is hidden in curve of leaf.

**Notes:** The bite of a garden spider is harmless to humans.

**Similar spiders:** None this size with plump, abdomen, red flashes on spiky legs.

**HABITAT** ANYWHERE IN AUST.

**FOOD** INSECTS

# Marine Invertebrates

Animals without backbones that live in the sea come in all shapes and sizes. The appearance of a marine invertebrate's body can vary depending on its life cycle and where it lives. Some live attached to a surface and look more like plants than animals. Most protect their soft bodies with tough, spiky skin, hard shells or external skeletons. It can be

These invertebrates resemble plants

difficult to identify a particular species; however, each main group has features not found in the other groups.

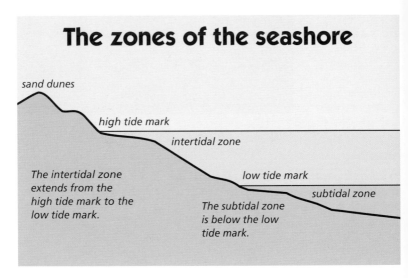

# The zones of the seashore

sand dunes

high tide mark

intertidal zone

The intertidal zone extends from the high tide mark to the low tide mark.

low tide mark

subtidal zone

The subtidal zone is below the low tide mark.

Marine invertebrates can be found from the highest point where waves splash the shore to the deepest trenches of the ocean floor. Most live within the first 30 metres of water where they crowd together in search of space, light and food.

# Marine invertebrate groups

There are eight main groups of invertebrates commonly found in Australian seas.

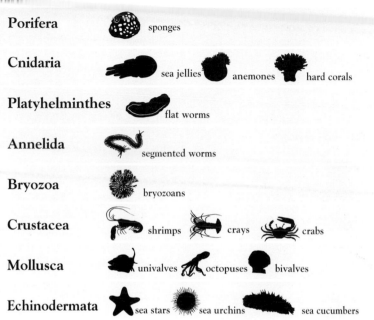

| | | |
|---|---|---|
| **Porifera** | sponges | |
| **Cnidaria** | sea jellies | anemones | hard corals |
| **Platyhelminthes** | flat worms | |
| **Annelida** | segmented worms | |
| **Bryozoa** | bryozoans | |
| **Crustacea** | shrimps | crays | crabs |
| **Mollusca** | univalves | octopuses | bivalves |
| **Echinodermata** | sea stars | sea urchins | sea cucumbers |

A group of animals called Ascidiacea, which includes sea squirts, has been included in this section because they can be mistaken for sponges. Ascidians are not classed as invertebrates because the larval stage has a very basic backbone or notochord that disappears in adulthood.

## Be aware
The bites, stings or spines of these animals can harm humans:

- Box Jelly
- Irukandji Jelly
- Cone shells
- Blue-ringed Octopus
- Sea urchins

 **hydroids**

Phylum *Cnidaria* (= stinging nettle animal)
Class *Hydrozoa* (= many headed serpent animal)

**Height:** 6–30 cm

**Description:** Attached colonies⁶ of hollow-bodied animals (polyps⁶) connected beneath limey skeletons. Skeleton forms a stalk with many side branches. Polyps can be seen along the branches. Can be a clump of delicate, fern-like branches or brittle mossy tufts of single stalks.

**Where found:** Temperate and tropical seas, all depths. Common in sheltered places below low water mark. In deep rock pools, on rocks, coral, seaweed, boat hulls and any submerged object.

**Habits:** Bottom-dwelling filter feeders. Food catching polyps have tentacles with stinging cells. Hydroids have a floating medusa⁶ life stage which buds off the colony to produce fertilised eggs which settle and grow into new polyps.

**Notes:** A Bluebottle is a floating hydroid colony of polyps suspended from a gas filled medusa. Fire coral is a hydroid with a hard skeleton and powerful stinging cells.

**Similar animals:** Bryozoans are smaller and not as feathery. Coralline algae have no polyps.

Solitary hydroid

Colonial hydroids

Phylum *Porifera* (= pore-bearer)

Tube sponge

Finger sponge and tube sponge

**Height:** 2–50 cm

**Width:** 6–50 cm

**Description:** Sac-shaped groups of animal cells. Mesh of fibres or sharp spicules[G] supports the cells. Colour varies. Texture can be firm, soft, rubbery or slimy. Shape can be branching, tube, finger, vase, round, honeycomb or encrusting.

**Where found:** Temperate and tropical seas, all depths. Common in shallow coastal and reef waters. In rock pools, crevices, under rocks and coral, on any firm surface.

Skeletons often wash up on sandy beaches.

**Habits:** Bottom-dwelling filter feeders. Cells with whip-like tails draw water and plankton through microscopic pores into hollow sac. Wastes are carried out through a large hole, the osculum. Sponges avoid direct sunlight. Some spp. bore into rocks.

**Notes:** Provide camouflage[G] and hiding places for other animals.

**Similar animals:** Ascidians have obvious intake and outflow holes.

# anemones

Phylum *Cnidaria* (= stinging nettle animal) Class *Zoantharia* (= flower animal) Order *Actinaria* (= with rays)

Sea whip anemone

**Diameter:** 1–50 cm

**Description:** Single, mobile polyps with no skeleton. Circles of stinging tentacles arranged in multiples of 6 surround the mouth. Has squat body column with sucker-like base. Tentacles can be withdrawn into body column. Some spp. have knobbed tentacles.

**Where found:** Temperate and tropical seas, all depths. Common in shallow water. In rock pools and crevices, under rocks and dead coral, on sand, sea whips and hermit crabs.

**Habits:** Feed on plankton, crustaceans and small fishes. Live alone, in clusters or colonies. Use base to creep over or hold onto any surface. Avoid direct sunlight. Some spp. burrow, others swim. Tropical spp. tend to be larger.

**Notes:** Anemonefish live among the stinging tentacles without being harmed. Hermit crabs put anemones on their shells for camouflage.

**Similar animals:** None.

Anemonefish in tentacles

# sea jellies

Phylum *Cnidaria* (= stinging nettle animal)
Class *Scyphozoa* (= cup-shaped animal)

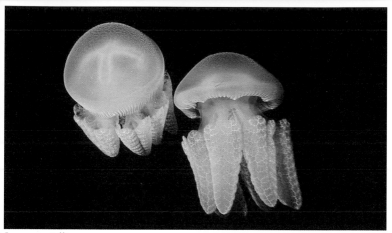

Large sea jellies

**Diameter:** 2–100 cm

**Description:** Hollow-bodied, planktonic animals (medusas). Body or bell is dome, saucer or box shaped and opaque to transparent. Stalked mouth surrounded by stinging tentacles located under bell. Light and gravity sensitive organs on bell edges.

**Where found:** Temperate and tropical water. Estuaries, inshore and open sea near surface. Often washed up on sandy beaches.

**Habits:** Free-floating animals transported by wind and currents. Pulsing movements of bell maintain and stabilise sea jelly's position in water. Tend to descend in rough weather. Feed on plankton, small fish. Some spp. have brief attached polyp stage.

**Notes:** Crustaceans and small fish often live under the bell.

**Similar animals:** Bluebottle medusa is not bell shaped or divided into sections.

271

# soft corals

Phylum *Cnidaria* (= stinging nettle animal) Class *Alcyonaria* (= polyp animal) Order *Alcyonacea* (= polyp animal)

**Height:** 10–150 cm

**Width:** 6–80 cm

**Description:** Colonial polyp animals protected by fleshy mass strengthened with spicules. Each polyp has eight hollow tentacles around a central mouth. Visible polyps can retract into mass and are connected to each other. Coloured mass can be lobed, folded or stoutly branched. Leathery or fleshy texture.

**Where found:** Temperate and tropical seas, all depths. Abundant in warm coastal and reef waters. Attached to rocks, coral and other hard surfaces.

**Habits:** Bottom-dwelling filter feeders. Polyps often extended during the day to feed on plankton.

**Notes:** Deepwater spp. are more rigid with a greater number of spicules.

**Similar animals:** Bryozoan branches are smaller and have geometric pattern.

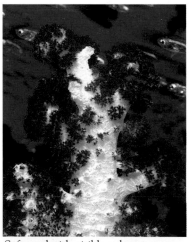

Soft coral with visible polyps

Encrusting soft coral

There are many species of soft coral, in various shapes, colours and sizes.

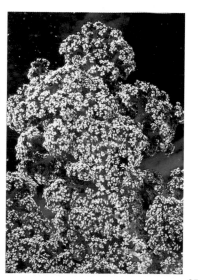 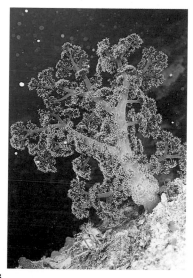

# sea pens

Phylum *Cnidaria* (= stinging nettle animal)
Class *Alcyonaria* (= polyp animal)  *Order Pennatulacea* (= plumed)

**Length:** To 1 m

**Description:** Feather-shaped or cylindrical colony of polyps. One large polyp forms central stalk. Smaller polyps attach directly to stalk or in rows on branches. Polyps arranged to face prevailing water current. Calcareous<sup>G</sup> spicules<sup>G</sup> support colony. White or cream; or yellowish-orange or pink.

**Where found:** On mud, sand or silt in shallow, sheltered bays; tropical and temperate seas.

**Habits:** Often found in groups. Polyps feed on plankton at night. Several species can retract into sediment during the day or when disturbed by water pressure changes in the animal's canals of central stalk.

**Notes:** Some spp. luminesce with pulses of light that radiate along the branches. Nudibranchs prey on some spp.

**Similar animals:** Sea whips have rigid skeletons. Soft corals have irregular branches.

# sea fans and whips

Phylum *Cnidaria* (= stinging nettle animal) Class *Alcyonaria* (= polyp animal) Order *Gorgonacea* (= snake haired)

**Height:** 20–300 cm

**Description:** Colonial polyps surrounded by rigid external skeleton. Polyps are short with central mouth and tentacles. Fans have a short main stem and latticed branches. A plate or clump of root-like extensions holds stem to bottom. Whips can be long, single stems or finely branched. Red, orange and yellow are common colours.

**Where found:** Temperate and tropical seas, all depths. Abundant in tropics below 10 m. Attached to any hard surface, especially near currents.

**Habits:** Bottom-dwelling plankton feeders. Polyps on most spp. can retract into skeleton. Fans grow in one direction in currents, in all directions in deep, calm water. Whips usually live in groups.

**Notes:** Other invertebrates live on or among gorgonian branches.

**Similar animals:** Hydroid branches are more delicate and feathery.

Sea fan

Long branching gorgonian

275

Vase Coral

Tree Coral

Bush Coral

Hard Coral

# hard corals

Phylum *Cnidaria* (= stinging nettle animal) Class *Zoantharia* (= flower animal) Order *Scleractinia* (= with hard rays)

**Diameter:** 0.5–30 cm solitary 10–500 cm colonial

**Description:** Single or colonial polyps which secrete hard cup-like skeleton. Corals are classified by the number and shape of the ridges inside the cup. Polyps can retract their stinging tentacles into the cup. Solitary corals are round or oval and not always attached. In colonial spp. the polyps are connected beneath the joined cups. Skeleton shapes can be encrusting, lobed, rounded, plate or branched.

**Where found:** Temperate and tropical seas, all depths. Reef building spp. need shallow, warm (20+°C) water.

**Habits:** Filter feeders attached to bottom. Most polyps extend at night to feed on plankton. Temperate spp. are smaller and more compact. Tropical spp. tend to be branching and reef building.

**Notes:** Single celled algae live in the tissues of many reef building polyps and provide them with food. Crown-of-thorns Sea Stars eat coral polyps.

**Similar animals:** Hydroid, bryozoan, and coralline algae skeletons are more brittle.

Branching staghorn coral

Free-living mushroom coral

277

Phylum *Platyhelminthes* (= flat worm)
Class *Turbellaria* (= little crowd)

**Length:** 1–5 cm

**Description:** Thin, flat, soft-bodied animals. Hair-like cilia⁶ cover body, edges usually rippled. Distinct head with one or more pairs of eyes and antenna-like tentacles. Mouth underneath near middle. Muscular tube (pharynx) connects mouth to finely branched gut. Tropical spp. tend to be more brightly coloured.

**Where found:** Temperate and tropical seas. Mainly intertidal⁶ pools and shallow water. Under rocks, on sand, rubble, rocks and seaweed.

**Habits:** Free-swimming bottom-dwellers. Characteristic gliding movements. Active predators of small invertebrates. Pharynx can be pushed out of mouth to grasp prey. Male and female reproductive systems present in each worm.

**Notes:** Some spp. live on or in sea cucumbers, urchins, molluscs, crabs and fish.

**Similar animals:** Nudibranchs have muscular foot and gill plumes.

Flat worm

# bristle worms

Phylum *Annelida* (= ringed animal)
Class *Polychaeta* (= many bristles)

**Length:** microscopic–1m free-moving spp. 5–25 cm tube/burrowing spp.

**Description:** Flexible worms with segmented bodies. Free-moving spp. have 2 head segments; one with eyes and tentacles, the other with mouth and sometimes jaws. Remaining segments have a pair of flaps with bristles (chaetae). Tube and burrowing spp. have modified head and reduced chaetae. Colourful head tentacles of tube worms can be threads, plumes or feathery whorls. Encrusting or single tubes built of sand, shell fragments, or secreted limestone.

**Where found:** Temperate and tropical seas, all depths. In sand, silt and mud of estuaries and beaches. Encrusting tubes on or under intertidal rocks. Below low water mark on rocks, in coral.

Feather duster tube worm

Bristle worm

**Habits:** Free-moving spp. swallow invertebrate prey whole. Tube spp. catch plankton. Tentacles are light sensitive and withdraw quickly.

**Notes:** Some spp. bore into bivalve shells.

**Similar animals:** None.

279

# crays

Phylum *Crustacea* (= shelled animal) Class *Malacostraca*
(= soft-shelled) Order *Decapoda* (= ten-footed)

**Length:** 20–100 cm

**Description:** Soft-bodied, segmented animals with a hard crust. This exoskeleton forms a heavy shield (carapace<sup>G</sup>) over head and upper body. Head has stalked eyes, 2 pairs of antennae and jaw-legs (maxillipeds) for feeding. Carapace and antennae can have spines. Gills at base of 5 pairs of jointed walking legs. Long abdomen has flattened swimming limbs and tail fan.

**Where found:** Temperate and tropical seas. Below low tide mark in crevices, caves, under overhangs.

**Habits:** Bottom-dwelling. Nocturnal predators of molluscs, worms and echinoderms. Usually feed in deep water. Move inshore to moult and breed. Females carry eggs under abdomen. Walk forward, but flick tail to shoot backwards.

**Notes:** Australian crays do not have a pair of large claws. Second pair of antennae in slipper lobsters and 'bugs' are flattened like a shield.

**Similar animals:** None.

Painted cray

Phylum *Crustacea* (= shelled animal) Class *Malacostraca* (= soft shelled) Order *Decapoda* (= ten-footed)

Cleaner shrimp

**Length:** 2–12 cm

**Description:** Long tailed decapods with segmented body and 5 pairs of jointed legs usually with claws (chela). First pair of claws often very large. Carapace extends between the stalked eyes to a sharp point. Colour varies, usually a regular pattern.

**Where found:** Temperate and tropical seas, all depths. Open sea, estuaries, lagoons, below low tide mark in rock and coral crevices, on seaweed, under intertidal rocks.

**Habits:** Can be plankton feeders, scavengers or predators. Sexes are separate. Most spp. carry eggs on abdomen. Some spp. live on or in other invertebrates. Some spp. travel in schools.

**Notes:** Deep sea spp. often bright red, some are luminescent. Cleaner spp. eat parasites living on fish.

**Similar animals:** None.

Burrowing shrimp

281

# crabs

Phylum *Crustacea* (= shelled animal) Class *Malacostraca* (= soft-shelled) Order *Decapoda* (= ten-footed)

Female crab carrying eggs

**Width:** 1–20+ cm

**Description:** Short-tailed decapods with broad, flattened carapaces. First pair of jointed legs often have large, brightly coloured claws. In some spp. fifth pair are modified for swimming or burrowing. Head has stalked eyes and short antennae. Colours usually match background.

**Where found:** Temperate and tropical seas, all depths. Estuaries, mangroves, mudflats, beaches; on or in sand, mud, silt. Under rocks in pools, among corals.

**Habits:** Bottom-dwelling. Characteristic sideways scuttle, can also swim and burrow. Large claws used for catching food, defence and courtship displays. Most are scavengers or prey on other invertebrates. Some sift food from ground leaving pellets or balls of sand or silt.

**Notes:** Some spp. live on or in other invertebrates, also on seaweeds.

This crab is camouflaged

# hermit crabs

Phylum *Crustacea* (= shelled animal) Class *Malacostraca* (= soft-shelled) Order *Decapoda* (= ten-footed)

Temperate red hermit crab

**Length:** 1–10 cm

**Description:** Crabs with long, soft body and hooked limbs to hold mollusc shells. No tail fan. Long antennae and stalked eyes. Three pairs of bristly, patterned legs visible. First pair have large claws, right usually larger than left. One claw often flattened to shield shell opening. Colours vary from bright red to dull olive.

**Where found:** Temperate and tropical seas. Intertidal rock pools. Rocky shores, coral reefs, sand patches below low tide mark.

**Habits:** Free-moving bottom-dwellers. Live in empty mollusc shells. Filter plankton, scavenge or prey on invertebrates. Each sp. prefers certain type of shell. Touches and probes empty shell before moving in.

**Notes:** One sp. burrows into soft rocks instead of using a shell.

Phylum *Mollusca* (= soft-bodied)
Class *Gastropoda* (= stomach-foot)

Cone shell

**Length:** 1–45 cm

**Description:** Soft-bodied molluscs protected by single shells. Shell is secreted by skin-like mantle⁶ which covers body. Muscular foot. Distinct head with eyes, tentacles and mouth. Tongue-like band of teeth (radula⁶). Horny plate (operculum) closes shell opening. Most spp. spiral or dome shaped. Colour and pattern varies in each sp.

**Where found:** Temperate and tropical seas. Beaches, mudflats, mangroves, estuaries, rocky shores, coral reefs. On sand patches, among rocks, coral, seaweeds and mangrove roots.

**Habits:** Free-moving, bottom-dwellers. Creeps or holds on with foot. Radula rasps off or drills into food. Can be predator, scavenger or grazing plant-eater.

**Notes:** Some planktonic spp. float beneath raft of bubbles.

**Similar animals:** Barnacles are feather-footed crustaceans surrounded by a case of hard plates.

Cowrie shell

# nudibranchs and sea hares

Phylum *Mollusca* (= soft-bodied) Class *Gastropoda* (= stomach-foot)
Orders *Nudibranchia* (= naked gills) *Aplysiomorpha* (= filthy form)

Nudibranch with plumed gills

Sea hare

**Length:** nudibranchs 2–12 cm sea hares up to 50 cm

**Description:** Slug-like gastropods. Shell absent or small and covered by mantle. Muscular foot. Mouth with radular teeth. Nudibranchs have flattened body, plumed branching gills or tufts on back. One pair of tentacles near mouth. Bright colours. Sea hares have 2 pairs of tentacles folded like rabbit ears. Skin flaps on sides of muscular foot. Dull colours.

**Where found:** Temperate and tropical seas. Estuarine flats, rocky shores, coral reefs. In shallow water especially in summer.

**Habits:** Free-moving, bottom-dwellers. Migrate to shallow water to breed. Sea hares lay strings of yellow or green eggs. They eat algae and seagrass. Nudibranchs graze on sponges and cnidarians.

**Notes:** Sea hares expel a purplish dye when threatened.

**Similar animals:** Flat worms usually thinner and smaller than nudibranchs.

# bivalves

Phylum *Mollusca* (= soft-bodied) Class *Bivalvia* (= 2 valves)

**Width:** 5–50 cm

**Description:** Soft-bodied molluscs with two-part, hinged shell. Two powerful muscles close shell. Muscular foot is tongue-like or absent. No head; gills sort food into mouth. Fleshy mantle covers body forming two siphons and gill cavity. Sensory spots along mantle edges.

**Where found:** Temperate and tropical seas, all depths. Attached to or under rocks and coral.

**Habits:** Attached or free-moving bottom-dwellers. Many spp. burrow. Some swim by opening and closing shell. Most feed on plankton.

**Notes:** Giant clams grow up to 1.5 m. Blue-green algae live in their mantle.

**Common examples:** Oysters, pippis, scallops.

Giant clam

# octopuses

Phylum *Mollusca* (= soft-bodied) Class *Cephalopoda* (= head-foot) Order *Octopoda* (= eight-footed)

Camouflaged octopus

**Length:** 7–40 cm

**Description:** Molluscs with short, rounded body and no shell. Mantle covers body and forms pouch and siphon⁶ at side of head. Two feathery gills inside pouch. Head has 2 lidless eyes. Eight tentacles with suckers, usually of equal length. Beaked mouth in centre of tentacles. Deep sea spp. have fins.

**Where found:** Temperate and tropical seas. In shallow water on rock or sand. In holes and crevices. Not common on coral reefs. Some open sea spp.

**Habits:** Bottom-dwelling, usually solitary. Nocturnal predators of bivalves, fish and crustaceans. Change colour rapidly to match background. Female guards eggs laid in strands or clusters in crevices.

**Notes:** Blue-ringed Octopuses sometimes hide in triton shells.

**Similar animals:** None.

Blue-ringed Octopus

 # squid

Phylum *Mollusca* (= soft-bodied) Class *Cephalopoda*
(= head-foot) Order *Teuthiodea* (= squid)

**Length:** 3–50 cm

**Description:** Molluscs with thin, flat, internal shell. Long, slender body with mantle flaps. Ten tentacles; 2 are longer, sometimes ending in hooks and not retractable. Eyes have no lids.

**Where found:** Temperate and tropical seas, all depths. Coastal and open sea.

**Habits:** Fast swimmers. Usually travel in schools. Feed on fish and crustaceans. Finger-shaped egg cases are attached to hard surfaces.

**Notes:** Giant deepwater squid grow up to 18 m. Schools of small squid are an important source of food for toothed whales.

**Similar animals:** None.

Squid using mantle flaps to swim

Phylum *Mollusca* (= soft-bodied) Class *Cephalopoda* (= head-foot) Order *Sepioidea* (= like black ink)

Giant Cuttlefish

**Length:** 5–30 cm

**Description:** Molluscs with short, flattened body. Skin flaps along each side. Rigid internal shell (cuttlebone). Ten tentacles; 2 usually longer with suckers on flattened end and retractable. Eyes have transparent cover and lids. Siphon under head.

**Where found:** Temperate and tropical seas. Prefer shallow coastal water. Some open sea spp. Cuttlebones often wash up on beaches and rocky shores.

**Habits:** Use fin-like flaps for slow swimming. Shoot water jet out of siphon to move quickly. Change colour and use clouds of ink to avoid predators. Feed on fish and crustaceans at night.

**Notes:** Egg clusters attached to rocks, seaweed and sponges.

**Similar animals:** None.

Cuttlebone

# bryozoans

Phylum *Bryozoa* (= moss animal)

Lacy bryozoan

**Diameter:** 0.1–100 cm

**Description:** Microscopic colonial animals with brain and simple nervous system. Mouth in centre of feathery tentacles. Open box of lime surrounds each body. Animals are connected through holes in the boxes, which are arranged in geometric rows like bricks in a wall. Colonies can be mossy tufts, thin crusts or lacy branches.

**Where found:** Temperate and tropical seas, all depths. Crevices, caves, overhangs, on or under any hard surface.

**Habits:** Colonies attached to bottom. Individuals are specialised for filtering plankton, cleaning, brooding larvae and forming joints or attachment branches. Individual animals cannot grow but collapse and regenerate[G] in winter.

**Notes:** Coloniser of bare surfaces.

**Similar animals:** Branching hydroids have visible polyps. Coralline algae do not have geometric pattern.

# feather stars

Phylum *Echinodermata* (= spiny-skinned) Class *Crinoidea*
(= lily-like) Order *Comatulida* (= long-haired)

**Diameter:** 10–25 cm

**Description:** Primitive animals with small, domed body of plates. Set of feathery, upward arms surround mouth on top of body. Arms have grooves and tube feet. Whorl of short, jointed arms (cirri) below body.

**Where found:** Temperate and tropical seas. In shallow water on any surface. Reef edges where current flows. On shady rock faces and among rocks at low tide in temperate waters.

**Habits:** Free-moving bottom-dwellers. Avoid direct sunlight. Do not move a lot, but can walk on cirri or flap arms to swim. Feed on plankton at night. Tube feet channel food into mouth. Can regenerate lost or damaged arms.

**Notes:** Small fish and crustaceans live among arms.

**Similar animals:** Basket stars are larger and have fern-like branches.

Feather star walking on cirri

Feather stars feed on plankton

# ⭐ sea stars

Phylum *Echinodermata* (= spiny-skinned)
Class *Asteroidea* (= star-like)

**Diameter:** 8–50 cm

**Description:** Tough-skinned animals each with 5 or more arms radiating from centre of body. Skin is embedded with flexible plates and spines. Tube feet with suckers in grooves under arms. Pore on top of body regulates water pressure in tube feet. Tiny, white gills and pincer-like organs between spines. Central mouth under body.

**Where found:** Temperate and tropical seas. Coral reefs and rocky bottoms below low tide. Estuaries and beaches under sand.

**Habits:** Use tube feet for walking and gripping prey. Carnivores feed on sponges, bryozoans, bivalves, worms and crustaceans. Other spp. eat decayed particles (detritus) found on rocks, sand and seaweed.

**Notes:** Can regenerate lost arms and new sea stars from body.

**Similar animals:** None.

Sea star

Long-armed sea star

Phylum *Echinodermata* (= spiny-skinned)
Class *Ophiuroidea* (= snake-like)

Brittle star uses its arms to move

**Diameter:** 10–75 cm

**Description:** Animals which have solid, flexible arms radiating from a distinct body disc. Arms can be smooth, spiny or branching but have no groove. Retractable tube feet have no suckers and are not obvious. Toothed mouth and water pressure pore under body.

**Where found:** Temperate and tropical seas. Below low tide under rocks and coral. On sand, mud, rocks, gravel. Sometimes found on kelp holdfasts⁶ and gorgonians.

**Habits:** Fast moving bottom-dwellers. Avoid direct sunlight. Tube feet catch food, arms push it into mouth. Most feed on detritus or prey on worms, crustaceans and bivalves.

**Notes:** Arms break off easily.

**Similar animals:** None.

Coiled arms of serpent star

Phylum *Echinodermata* (= spiny-skinned)
Class *Echinoidea* (= spine-like)

Slate Pencil Urchin

Short-spined sea urchin

**Diameter:** 5–25 cm

**Description:** Animals with round or flat case of close-fitting, rigid plates. Rows of swivelling spines and tube feet with suckers between plates. Spines can be long, short, fine or thick. Central mouth under body has 5 wedge-shaped grinding teeth.

**Where found:** Temperate and tropical seas, all depths. On soft and hard bottoms. In rock pools and below low tide between rocks and coral, in hollows.

**Habits:** Free-moving bottom-dwellers. Active at night. Feed on seaweed, bryozoans and sponges. Use tube feet and bottom spines to walk. Tend to cluster in groups. Some spp. burrow in sand.

**Notes:** Only invertebrate with a chewing mouth. Some deep sea spp. have luminescent organs.

**Similar animals:** None.

Phylum *Echinodermata* (= spiny-skinned) Class *Holothuriodea*

**Length:** 5-50 cm

**Description:** Sausage-shaped animals with tough skin. Plates reduced to tiny bones poking through skin. Five bands of tube feet along body. Three bottom rows used for moving. Mouth at one end with branching tentacles and no teeth.

**Where found:** Temperate and tropical seas. Larger and more common in tropics. Below low tide on sand or silt patches between rocks and coral. In hollows and crevices.

**Habits:** Free-moving bottom-dwellers. Can be filter feeders or predators. Some spp. digest organic material from the sand they swallow. Can regenerate whole digestive system.

**Notes:** Worms, crustaceans and fish live inside body.

**Similar animals:** One sp. mimics a nudibranch. Sea slugs have antennae.

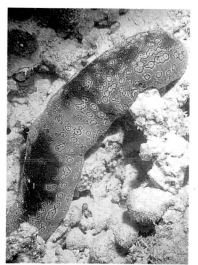

Bottom-feeding sea cucumber

Sea cucumber with feeding tentacles

**simple ascidians**

Phylum *Chordata* (= having a chord)
Class *Ascidiacea* (= like a bag)

**Height:** 2–20 cm

**Description:** Single, sac-like animals with fibrous skin (tunic). Two siphons create water current across sieve-like gill⁶ slits. Tunic can be leathery or gelatinous, sometimes delicate. Often colourful with other animals growing on tunic.

**Where found:** Temperate and tropical seas, all depths. Common intertidally and in shallow water. On rocks, coral, sand, mud, boats and wharves.

**Habits:** Adult is attached to bottom and filters plankton. Free-swimming larvae has tail with nerve chord and strong rod. Tail, chord and rod disappear when it settles head first and grows into adult.

**Notes:** Eggs and sperm are released into water.

**Similar animals:** None.

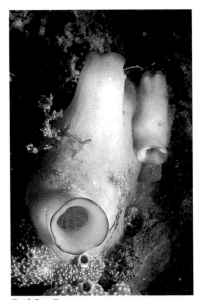
Red Sea Squirt

A group of stalked ascidians

# compound ascidians

Phylum *Chordata* (= having a chord)
Class *Ascidiacea* (= like a bag)

**Width:** 10–50 cm

**Description:** Colony of small ascidians with connected bodies. Bases can be joined by central stalk or root-like branches. Colony can share one tunic, but animals have own siphons. Other spp. share tunic and common outflow siphon.

**Where found:** Same as simple ascidians.

**Habits:** Bottom-dwelling filter feeders. Colonies grow by adding new animals. Eggs are fertilised inside colony. Larvae develop in the same manner as simple ascidians.

**Notes:** Ascidian larvae are first group of marine animals to show the beginnings of a backbone which is found in all vertebrates.

**Similar animals:** Sponges do not have regular pattern of holes.

Colonial ascidians share tunic

Magnificent Ascidian

# Wildlife conservation

The more we learn about Australia's wild animals, the more we appreciate their value and uniqueness. While Australia has an amazing diversity of wildlife, it does not have large numbers of each species. When we change the land and its vegetation to suit human purposes, we threaten the survival of these remarkable animals.

Exploring our marine environment

Australia has the world's worst record for plant and animal extinctions. At present some 1500 Australian plant and animal species are in danger of becoming extinct because of vegetation clearance and the introduction of animals and plants from other countries.

Research increases knowledge

When we look after the land and its native animals, we help maintain the biological diversity that makes life on Earth possible.

Learning about our wildlife

A new experience

# Recommended reading

## Australian Wildlife

SLATER, P, 2000, *Encyclopedia of Australian Wildlife*, Steve Parish Publishing, Brisbane.
SLATER, P, 2002, *Ark Australia Series (4 titles)*, Steve Parish Publishing, Brisbane.
SLATER, P, 2002, *WOW Series (4 titles)*, Steve Parish Publishing, Brisbane.

## Mammals

CRONIN, L, 1991, *Key Guide to Australian Mammals*, Reed, Sydney.
SLATER, P, 1997, *Amazing Facts About Australian Mammals*, Steve Parish Publishing, Brisbane.
STRAHAN, R, 1992, *Encyclopedia of Australian Animals: Mammals*, Angus & Robertson, Sydney.
STRAHAN, R, 2002, *(ed.)The Mammals of Australia*, Reed New Holland, Sydney.

## Frogs & Reptiles

BARKER, J, *et al.*, 1995, *A Field Guide to Australian Frogs*, Surrey Beatty & Sons, Sydney.
COGGER, HG, 2000, *Reptiles & Amphibians of Australia*, 6th edn, Reed New Holland, Sydney.
EHMANN, H, 1992, *Encyclopedia of Australian Animals: Reptiles*, Angus & Robertson, Sydney.
SLATER, P, 1997, *Amazing Facts About Australian Frogs and Reptiles*, Steve Parish Publishing, Brisbane.
TYLER, MJ, 1992, *Encyclopedia of Australian Animals: Frogs*, Angus & Robertson, Sydney.

## Birds

LINDSAY, TR, 1992, *Encyclopedia of Australian Animals: Birds*, Angus & Robertson, Sydney.
MORCOMBE, M, 2000, *Field Guide to Australian Birds*, Steve Parish Publishing, Brisbane.
READER'S DIGEST, 1982, *Reader's Digest Complete Book of Australian Birds*, Reader's Digest, Sydney.
SLATER, P, 1997, *Amazing Facts About Australian Birds*, Steve Parish Publishing, Brisbane.
SLATER, P, *et al.*, 2002, *The Slater Field Guide to Australian Birds*. Reed New Holland, Sydney.

## Insects & Spiders

BRUNET, B, 1994, *The Silken Web*. Reed Books, Sydney.
HADLINGTON, PW, JOHNSTON, JA, 1990, *Introduction to Australian Insects*, UNSWP, Sydney.
MAIN, B, 1984, *Spiders,*Collins, Sydney.
SLATER, P, 1997, *Amazing Facts About Australian Insects and Spiders*, Steve Parish Publishing, Brisbane.
ZBOROWSKI, P, STORY, R, 1995, *A Field Guide to Insects in Australia*, Reed Books, Sydney.

## Marine Life

ALLEN , GR, STEENE, R, 1994, *Indo-Pacific Coral Reef Guide*, Tropical Reef Research, Singapore.
EDGAR, GJ, 2000, *Australian Marine Life; the Plants and Animals of Temperate Waters*, Reed New Holland, Sydney.
SLATER, P, 1997, *Amazing Facts about Australian Marine Life*, Steve Parish Publishing, Brisbane.

## Fish

CALCUTT, R, 1992, *Ron Calcutt's Complete Book of Fishing*, Simon and Schuster.
COLEMAN, N, 1980, *Australian Sea Fishes South of 30°S*, Doubleday, Sydney.
COLEMAN, N, 1981, *Australian Sea Fishes North of 30°S*, Doubleday, Sydney.
GOMMON, MF, *et al.*, 1994, *The Fishes of Australia's South Coast*, State Print, Adelaide.

# Glossary <sup>G</sup>

**aestivate** To become inactive in unfavourable conditions.

**algae** Group of plants, some single celled; some seaweeds; the "pastures" of the sea.

**anal** Of or near final opening of digestive tract.

**antivenom** Substance that counters the effect of venom.

**baleen** Fringed plates on upper jaws of toothless whales.

**barbels** Fleshy tentacle-like feeler usually near the mouth.

**bask** Expose body to warmth.

**book-lungs** Pair of breathing structures in arachnids. Each book-lung is a cavity that contains double-walled leaves between which blood circulates.

**calcareous** Containing or coated with calcium carbonate; chalky.

**callosities** Areas of thick or hardened skin.

**camouflage** To blend with surround-ings through colours and patterns.

**canine** Pointed, cone-shaped tooth.

**carapace** Hard shield covering top and sides of body.

**carnivore** Animal that eats animals.

**carrion** Dead flesh.

**cephalothorax** Combined head and thorax.

**cerci** Paired appendages at tip of abdomen.

**chelicerae** Paired mouth appendages forming fangs.

**chrysalis** Butterfly pupa.

**cilia** Thread-like projections which beat rhythmically.

**colony** Group of animals of same species living together.

**concave** Curving inwards.

**convex** Curving outwards.

**crustaceans** Invertebrates with external skeletons and jointed limbs; crab, prawn, crayfish.

**display** Behaviour used to communicate with other animals.

**disruptive coloration** Patterns that break up the shape of an animal's body.

**dominant** First in importance.

**dorsal** On the back.

**echinoderms** Spiny-skinned marine animals.

**echolocation** Use of high-pitched sounds to locate objects.

**elongate** Long in comparison to width.

**embryo** Animal in early stage of development.

**fertile** Able to reproduce.

**fledged** Of a young bird, having the feathers of an adult.

**flukes** Flat parts of a marine mammal's tail.

**forage** To search for food.

**fused teeth** Joined teeth forming single cutting or grinding surface.

**gape** Distance between jaws.

**gill slits** Openings behind the head through which water is forced after oxygen has been extracted.

**glandular** Containing glands.

**habitat** The place where an animal or plant lives.

**herbivore** Animal that eats plants.

**hive** Structure built by colonial bees.

**holdfast** Root-like anchoring structure on seaweeds.

**hovers** Remains airborne without moving forward.

**incubate** Keep eggs at constant temperature until they hatch.

**infertile** Unable to reproduce.

**inshore waters** Waters washing the shore.

**instar** One growth stage between moults.

**intertidal** Area between low and hide tide marks.

**irregular** Each part different from other parts.

**joey** Young macropod; kangaroo, wallaby. Also young Koala.

**keeled** Bearing a central ridge.

**krill** Small crustaceans.

**larva** Development stage between egg and adult.

**mantle** Fold of skin covering mollusc's body.

**medusa** Free-moving, bell-shaped form of sea jelly.

**megabat** Large fruit-eating bat.

**membrane** Thin tissue or skin.

**microbat** Small, insect-eating bat.

**moult** To shed and regrow skin, feathers, fur, hair.

**nymph** Young stage of insect whose life history has many gradual changes.

**noseleaf** Skin growth on snout of microbat.

**ovipositor** Organ through which female insect lays eggs.

**parasites** Animals that live on or in other animals from which they feed.

**pectoral** On sides of body near head.

**pedipalps** Appendages on either side of mouth.

**plankton** Plants and animals that drift in sea water; usually microscopic.

**plastron** Ventral part of a turtle shell.

**plumes** Ornamental feathers used for display.

**pods** Closely-knit groups of swimming creatures.

**polyp** Attached form of cnidarian having a hollow body, and mouth surrounded by tentacles.

**predator** Animal that kills and eats animals.

**preening** Putting feathers in order.

**prehensile** Able to grasp.

**pupa** Inactive stage between larva and adult.

**radula** Gastropod's tongue-like band of teeth.

**range** Geographical area in which a plant or animal occurs.

**regenerate** To regrow lost body parts.

**roost** To settle down to sleep.

**scavenger** Animal that feeds on dead organic matter.

**scute** Sharply ridged scale.

**sensory pore** Small opening which senses conditions in the environment, as along the lateral line.

**siphon** Tube or canal.

**solitary** Living alone.

**species** Group of animals that can mate and produce fertile offspring.

**speculum** Patch of coloured feathers on pigeon's wing.

**spicules** Tiny, glass-like objects embedded in body mass.

**spinnerets** Spinning organs.

**spiracle** Opening behind shark's eye, used for breathing.

**status** Indication of whether numbers in a species are increasing or decreasing.

**subspecies** Further division of a species.

**subtidal** Below low tide level.

**terminal** At the end of the body.

**territory** Area claimed and defended for food and breeding.

**torpid** State of reduced activity.

**toxin** Poison.

**tube feet** Short, hollow limbs connected to water canal system in echinoderms.

**tubercle** Small, cone-shaped bump.

**tubers** Underground plant stems.

**tympanum** Hearing organ.

**venom** Poison of animal origin.

**venomous** Poisonous.

**vent** Final opening of digestive tract.

**ventral** Of the belly; underneath.

**vertical** Upright; at right angles to the horizontal line.

**vulnerable** Not protected.

**weaning** Time when mammals cease suckling.

# Index and checklist